THE NEW TESTAMENT FOR TODAY

THE
NEW TESTAMENT
FOR TODAY

A. M. HUNTER

THE SAINT ANDREW PRESS
EDINBURGH

First published in 1974 by
THE SAINT ANDREW PRESS
121 George Street Edinburgh
© A. M. Hunter 1974

ISBN 0 7152 0309 6

Printed in Great Britain by
Robert MacLehose and Company Limited, Glasgow
Printers to the University of Glasgow

Contents

Preface

'A theological Rolls Royce' someone called a learned tome
which a friend of mine had written. He would have pronounced this one a Mini-Minor. But Rolls Royces are
beyond most people's purses, take some maintaining and
controlling, and are hard to park. The Mini costs a great
deal less, is easy to handle, and will go places where a
'transport of delight' like a Rolls has no hope of going. At
any rate it is my hope that this theological Mini-Minor
will 'transport' into the New Testament's 'realms of gold'
many ordinary folk who would turn away from a Rolls
with a sigh or shrug of despair.

It does not introduce individually all twenty-seven
books of the New Testament; but, after a general look at
the New Testament library, it picks out ten of the chief
books for special study, including two of the hardest,
Hebrews and Revelation. And who knows I may so whet
some readers' appetites that, like Oliver Twist, they will
ask for more?

Small though the book is, I have tried in it to reflect the
findings of modern scholarship, to avoid theological
jargon, and to show that the New Testament still contains
'a Word from the Beyond for our human predicament.'

Most of the material in the book may now be had also
in cassette form from the Saint Andrew Press.

For reading the proofs I am yet again indebted to my leal friend and neighbour in Ayr, the Reverend David G. Gray, once of St Peter's, Dundee.

A. M. HUNTER

1. Why study the New Testament?

In this short work we are going to study some, but not all, of the chief books of the New Testament. But, at the outset, we must face the question 'Why?' What do we find in the New Testament that we can find nowhere else?

The best way to begin is to consider two wrong — or, rather, inadequate — answers.

First, then, should we study it for its fine literature? From time to time we are told by our literary experts that the Bible, as literature, is on a par with Shakespeare. So it is. The Bible, as it comes to us in the glorious (if sometimes archaic) English of the Authorized Version of 1611, is our supreme book of English prose. Read the lament of David for Saul and Jonathan (2 Sam. 1), or the 40th chapter of Isaiah, or the 15th of Luke's Gospel with its story of the father and his two sons, or St Paul's hymn about Christian love in 1 Cor. 13, or the roll-call of the heroes of faith in Hebrews 11, and then tell me where you will find anything to excel them in power and beauty. And yet, though this is one reason why we cannot afford to neglect the Bible, it is not *the* reason why we Christians account it the greatest book in the world. For, after all, the Bible does not contain all the world's great literature. Great literature you may find in other places — in Shakespeare and many another. Yet there is something in the Bible you will not find elsewhere.

Let us try again. You often hear the Bible called 'the

2 THE NEW TESTAMENT FOR TODAY

Good Book'. A book about goodness? Is it as a text-book on the good life that we ought to study it? Well, every serious-minded person is interested in the problem of right living and would fain know how best he may live out his time on earth. Is it then because we have in the Bible a supreme text-book on morals that we ought to study it?

Once again, the answer must be 'No', though now we are 'getting hotter', as the children say. Of course there is moral light and leading in the Bible — plenty of it. The Ten Commandments (Exod. 20), for example. If they are pretty old by now, they are emphatically not out of date: 'You shall not commit murder. You shall not commit adultery. You shall not steal. You shall not give false evidence against your neighbour.' Then the New Testament contains the Sermon on the Mount (Matt. 5–7), generally regarded as the supreme utterance on the moral life. If it is moral light that we are after, there is nothing to match the Sermon. Yet, great as it is, you can get noble moral teaching outside the covers of the Bible. This is still not *the* reason why Christians believe, with Sir Walter Scott, that 'there is but one Book'.

What then do we find in the Bible that we find in no other book? We find 'the Word from the Beyond for our human predicament'.

Consider this. When, in time of sorrow or disaster, men and women turn to the Bible, what they are seeking is not fine literature or moral light and leading. No, perplexed by the mystery of this strange but lovely world, beset by sin and suffering, and knowing that in no long time they must set out for that 'undiscovered country from whose bourn no traveller returns', they want an assurance that goes further and deeper than that. They want an assurance that in all their guilt and grief the almighty Being who made the world really and veritably cares about all his creatures — nay more, that he has done something for them, something great and adequate, something worthy of a God. 'When I go to church on Sunday,' a man once said to me, 'I want to hear what God has done for his world, and what he can do in and through me.' Now it is just this message, this assurance, this 'Word from the Beyond for our human predicament', that the Bible claims to give.

For the Bible declares (and now we are at the answer) not only that there is a God who cares about his world, but that once in history he came right down into it as a man, to show us what he is like, and then died as a man to bind us to himself for ever.

This is the climax of the story which the Bible tells: God's coming into our world in the person of Christ his Son. For, to use one technical term, the Bible is the record of *a progressive revelation*. It tells how God revealed himself to men, not all at once but bit by bit as they were able to receive him. The story of that revelation reaches away back to God's call of a man named Abraham from Ur of the Chaldees. 'In you,' God promised him, 'shall all the families of the earth be blessed' (Gen. 12: 3). It goes on to tell how God chose a special people, Israel, in order to reveal himself to them that they, in turn, might be 'a light for revelation to the Gentiles'; how God spoke to Israel through gifted men called prophets and disciplined them through the centuries by judgment and blessing; how he kindled in their hearts the hope of a future when he would crown his revelation of himself by inaugurating a 'new covenant' (or 'dispensation') with them (Jer. 31: 31ff.); and how, when the time came, he did just this by sending his own Son into the world, to live and die and rise again for men's saving, and so be 'Immanuel', God with us, to the end of time.

The claim of the Bible is therefore that in Christ the ultimate meaning of this mysterious universe has been revealed — that behind it is not an inscrutable Fate but an almighty Father; that his will is that men should live in fellowship with him, both here and hereafter; and that he has given his Son and his helping Spirit to make all this possible.

Here, however, somebody may object: 'What right have we to suppose that the Hebrews and, after them, the Christians have any monopoly of religious truth, of genuine divine revelation? Is it not a bit presumptuous to claim that God, in revealing himself, did so to a small section of the human race, while the rest was left in darkness?' A good question!

But, in order to defend the Christian religion, we do not need to assert that the other world-religions are devoid of all divine truth. The New Testament does not in fact do so. (St Paul, for example, says that men may perceive God's invisible nature from his created works and that God has not left non-Christians without some clue to his character. *See* Rom. 1: 19f, and Acts 14: 17.) Yet when we consider the real possibilities, only three world-religions come into serious reckoning: the religion of the Bible, the religion of Mohammed (Islam), and the religion of Buddha.

But Mohammedanism is really a sort of petrified Judaism, the Allah of the Koran being a poor copy of the God of the Bible — a kind of almighty Sultan, and certainly not the God and Father of Christ. On the other hand, Buddhism is basically a system of self-culture without divine help, not a religion — a self-revelation of

God — in our sense of the word: it can get along tolerably well without the idea of God. Ultimately, therefore, it is not a matter of choosing among the religions. The real issue is the religion of the Bible — or none at all.

So we come back to the claim of the New Testament, as the fulfilment of the Old, that in Christ we have God's saving light for a dark world. Of course it is a tremendous claim to make — so tremendous that some cannot believe it. But there are others (about a thousand millions now in the world) who do believe it, and not only believe it but try to shape their lives by it. The solution to the riddle of the world lies not in Karl Marx and *Das Kapital* (as the Communist holds) but in Jesus Christ and the New Testament; this is the Christian claim. To accept it is not to have all life's mysteries solved at one stroke. Mysteries there will always be this side of eternity. (Here 'we see in a mirror dimly', says St Paul, and 'know only in part'. Only hereafter shall we know fully. *See* 1 Cor. 13: 9–13.) But to those who are humble enough to accept God's Good News in Christ, they will be mysteries not of darkness but of *light*. In Christ his only Son God has given us enough light to keep us trusting, and by that light we travel 'till travelling days are done'.

Now, before we close our first study, a word about the value of modern translations of the scriptures.

For all its literary splendours the AV (Authorized Version, or 'King James', as the Americans call it), made away back in 1611, is now inevitably dated and in places obscure and misleading. Thus, in Matt. 6: 25, it makes Jesus say, 'Take no thought for your life'. In 1611 this meant 'Don't worry'. Thus it is reported of a certain queen of England that 'she died of taking thought', i.e. not of over-working her brain but of worry. Nowadays 'take no thought for your life' might seem to forbid any foresight for the future. Or take Rom. 1: 13. Writing to the Christians in Rome about his forthcoming visit to them, Paul says 'I was let hitherto'. 'Let' here does not mean 'permitted' but 'prevented' (like a 'let ball' in tennis).

These two simple examples will show the advantages of a modern translation of the New Testament, particularly in Paul's letters where the Authorized Version is often unclear. For our purpose the two best ones are the RSV (which is short for Revised Standard Version) and the NEB (which is short for New English Bible). Both harvest the gains of modern scholarship but in different ways.

The special merit of the RSV is that, while it retains most of the glorious cadences of the AV, it gets rid of the archaisms and obscurities and is more accurate. Instead of 'Take no thought for your life' it has 'Be not anxious for your life', and instead of 'I was let hitherto' it has 'Thus far I have been prevented'.

The special merit of the NEB is that it is not a revision of a seventeenth century classic but a completely new translation into twentieth century English. Intelligibility for the modern reader is its chief aim. Your literary man may still prefer the AV to the NEB, but for accuracy, clarity and modernity the NEB is superior. Thus (whether you like it or not) the NEB's 'Bring us not to the test' is better than the AV's 'Lead us not into temptation'. This might suggest that, in Jesus' view, God may entice men into doing evil, which cannot be true of one who said 'None is good but God alone' (Mark 10: 18). So also, in the parable of the Prodigal Son, where the AV has 'The younger son gathered all together', the NEB more accurately translates 'turned the whole of his share into cash'.

Each translation therefore has its merits. If you hanker

after the glories of the AV, but without its obscurities, the book for you is the RSV, recently recognized by the three great churches of Christendom as *The Common Bible*, a version of the scriptures on which they can all agree. If you wish to get right away from Elizabethan English and read the Bible in contemporary speech, you will choose the NEB. But, RSV or NEB, the important thing is to get back to the Bible.

FOR DISCUSSION

1. 'The New Testament (or 'Covenant') lies hidden in the Old, and the Old is made plain in the New,' said St Augustine. Study Isa. 53 and Jer. 31: 31–34 and consider how these two Old Testament prophecies were fulfilled in Christ's life and death and resurrection.

2. Compare the Beatitudes (Matt. 5: 3–10) in the RSV and the NEB. Which translation do you prefer, and why?

Note: 'Blessed' or 'blest' does not mean simply 'happy': it means 'divinely happy', that is, enjoying the favour of God. Observe also that 'Heaven' in the Beatitudes is (like our use of the word 'Providence') another way of saying 'God'.

2. What's in the New Testament

In this second chapter our aim is to get an overall idea of what is in the New Testament. But before we do this, we must discuss two matters, the first of which is the original language of the New Testament.

A man once entered a bookshop and asked for a copy of the New Testament in Greek. After searching his shelves the bookseller reported back. 'I'm very sorry, sir,' he said, 'We've got the New Testament in French, and the New Testament in German, and the New Testament in Latin, but they don't seem, yet, to have translated it into Greek.'

The point of this story is, I'm sure, obvious. The language in which the New Testament was first written, was Greek, and the bookseller was nearly nineteen centuries behind the times. But why Greek?

Our Lord was born a Jew, not a Greek. His mother-tongue — the tongue in which he preached and prayed — was Aramaic, which is a kind of Hebrew. When he addressed his heavenly Father, he said not 'Pater' (which is Greek) but 'Abba' (which is Aramaic).

Well, here is the reason. The New Testament was written in Greek because 1900 years ago the international language of the time was Greek, much as English is today. This international Greek wasn't quite the polished Greek which they had used in Greece four or five centuries before Christ was born. It was the 'common' Greek which the great king Alexander of Macedon (in northern Greece) and his armies had spread all over the lands they conquered: a simpler, more colloquial Greek — called 'common Greek', not because it was necessarily bad Greek but because it was the Greek in common use.

You may guess how important this was for the first apostles. Nowadays when a missionary enters a foreign country, his first task is to sit down and learn the local lingo. Christ's missionaries were spared this huge inconvenience. Wherever they went, in the towns of Syria, in the highlands of Asia Minor, or in the streets of Corinth or Rome, they could count on finding people who knew Greek.

So much then for the original language. Before we come to the New Testament books themselves, I must say a word about 'the Gospel before the Gospels'.

In the beginning, remember, there were no Gospels or Epistles, in fact, no New Testament at all. Jesus, who left nothing in writing, was crucified in the year AD 30. Our earliest New Testament book was written about AD 50. Thus a gap of some twenty years separates the first preaching of the Gospel from the first book about it. How was the Gospel preached during these two decades?

Scholars call this time 'the period of the oral tradition', the time when the Gospel was transmitted from mouth to mouth by those who had been eye-witnesses of Jesus. By studying certain statements in Paul's letters (e.g. 1 Cor. 15: 3–7) and the Acts of the Apostles (e.g. Acts 10: 36–43) we may roughly reconstruct the outline of the preached Gospel (the Greek word for it is *kērygma*, 'proclamation') of those earliest days. This is what is meant by 'the Gospel before the Gospels'.[1]

[1] The classical study of this is C. H. Dodd's *The Apostolic Preaching* (1936).

Suppose you and I had been in the audience when one of the first apostles was speaking. What would have been the burden of his discourse? Nothing less than that God had at last fulfilled Israel's age-old hope of divine redemption. A reporter's summary of the apostle's preaching would have read something like this:

> 'The prophecies are fulfilled, and God's New Age has begun.
> The Messiah, born of David's line, has come.
> He is Jesus of Nazareth who, as God's Servant Son,
> Went about doing good and healing by God's power,
> Died for men's sins according to the scriptures,
> Was raised by God on the third day,
> Is now exalted to God's right hand,
> And will come in glory for judgment.
> Therefore let all who hear repent, believe and be baptized for the forgiveness of their sins and the gift of the Holy Spirit.'

Such, in brief, was the earliest Gospel. When men asked questions about this man Jesus, who was somehow Mary's son and God's, the apostles would tell them stories of the wonderful things Jesus had done while on earth: how he had healed the sick, and stilled the storm and cast out devils, and made dead men come alive again. They would also recall the wonderful words he had spoken, not least those parables about God's dawning Kingdom, or Reign, which Jesus had used to tell men about its nature and to challenge them to decision for or against God's great saving purpose.

At first, then, the Christians felt no need for books about Jesus. There were hundreds of people still living who could speak of Jesus as they remembered him, and to whom

Jesus, though his bodily presence was now withdrawn, was yet the most real presence in their lives.

Thus the years went by as the Gospel 'flew like hallowed fire from soul to soul' and from land to land; and one by one the eye-witnesses began, in apostolic phrase, 'to fall asleep', so that the number of those who had known Jesus in the days of his flesh grew ever smaller. It was then that the Christians began to feel acutely the need for written records of the works and words of Jesus.

So, about a generation after Jesus had died and risen, came the first written Gospel. Composed in Rome about AD 65, it was the work of John Mark, the friend of Peter and Paul. In the next thirty years followed the three others — Matthew, Luke and John — all telling basically the same story but writing with different readers in view: St Matthew for Jewish Christians, St Luke mostly for Gentile Christians and St John — well, for the wider world of men generally.

The New Testament had begun to be. Yet the Gospels were not the first Christian documents. Before Mark wrote the earliest one, Peter, Paul and other apostles were preaching the Gospel in many places and founding new churches. These new congregations often ran into trouble and needed guidance. What more natural than that they should appeal to Peter, Paul and others for help? So the apostles wrote letters of counsel, encouragement, or rebuke to Christians in Galatia, Thessalonica, Corinth, Philippi, Colossae, and so on. These letters were read aloud at church meetings, and were copied and exchanged with sister churches. Thus there grew up little collections of apostolic letters. These are the Epistles in our New Testament.

Most of the Gospels and Epistles were written between

AD 50 and 100; but not till about AD 200 did the New Testament take roughly the shape it has today. Why and how the Church at large decided that twenty-seven books should make up the New Testament 'Canon' — that is, the list of books accepted by Christians as authoritative for faith and life — is a long story into which we cannot go here. It is sufficient to say that they had a good many writings to choose from and that they were guided to choose the best.

Now let us take a quick look at the twenty-seven books of the New Testament. They fall into four classes:

(1) Four Gospels;
(2) A book of church history;
(3) Twenty-one Epistles, and
(4) An apocalypse.

This is their order in our New Testament, but it is not the order in which they were originally written. If we were to arrange the books in their *chronological* order, we should have to start with Paul's letters, written roughly between AD 50 and 62.

From a literary point of view the New Testament might be called 'a mixed bag'. First we have four books called Gospels telling the story of the earliest preached Gospel — how God had inaugurated his Kingdom, or saving Rule, in the life, death and resurrection of Jesus. After the Gospels comes a book of church history, the Acts of the Apostles, written by Dr Luke, the author of the third Gospel. Acts serves as a bridge between the Gospels and the rest of the New Testament, for in it we meet men and women who, though Christ's bodily presence has been withdrawn, know beyond all doubt that he is alive and present with them, through the Holy Spirit, wherever they go.

Next follow the twenty-one Epistles, though 'Epistle' is a broad label covering everything from a short private letter like Philemon to a massive theological treatise like Romans. Thirteen Epistles are ascribed to Paul. Romans, his most important, stands first in our New Testament. From Paul's letters we pass to the catholic, or general, epistles: Hebrews, James, the letters of Peter, John, and Jude.

Finally comes 'the Revelation of St John the Divine', as the Authorized Version calls it. It can be a very puzzling book to the ordinary reader until he is given the proper key to its interpretation. Once he gets this, he discovers that it is all about the judgment and victory of God, that it carries a message for all Christians who have to live in times of crisis, and that it makes a superb ending to the New Testament.

Now we have a rough idea of the New Testament's contents. In the next chapter we shall turn to the earliest Gospel.

FOR DISCUSSION

1. 'Christianity is first and foremost a Gospel, a proclamation to the world of something God has done for man in Christ' (T. W. Manson). If the heart of the Gospel is the Cross on the Hill and the Empty Tomb, where does the teaching of the Sermon on the Mount come in?

2. 'It needs the whole of the New Testament to show who Christ is' (James Denney). Why is it not enough to confine ourselves to the four Gospels?

3. The Earliest Gospel (Mark)

In the winter of AD 64 there broke out in Rome a great fire
which many blamed on the mad Emperor Nero. Looking
round for a suitable scapegoat, the authorities picked
on the new sect of the Christians who were highly un-
popular. There followed a reign of terror, and among
its victims were the two Christian leaders, Peter and
Paul.

Shortly after, a little book appeared in Rome with the
title 'the Gospel of Jesus Christ the Son of God'. It was the
earliest written Gospel and, according to the unanimous
tradition of the Church, the work of John Mark, a native
of Jerusalem and the friend of Peter and Paul. Possibly his
mother's house in Jerusalem was the scene of the Last
Supper; at any rate, it became a regular meeting-place
for the earliest Christians (Acts 12: 12).

If Mark was not one of the chosen twelve disciples, he
probably knew Jesus during the last period of his ministry,
in Jerusalem. In Mark 14: 51 reference is made to a young
man who escaped the arresting posse in the Garden of
Gethsemane only by leaving his linen garment behind him.
In the tremendous drama of Jesus' passion it seems a very
trifling incident, hardly worth recording. Imagine a
modern press reporter describing a terrible railway disaster
and then inserting this sentence: 'Just then Mr John Smith
lost his handkerchief.' As pointless is this verse in Mark's
Gospel — unless it refers to Mark himself — is his own

modest signature in the corner of his Gospel, his own quiet way of saying, 'I was there.'

What else do we know about Mark? From Acts we learn that about AD 47 he accompanied Barnabas his cousin and Paul on their first missionary journey in the role of 'assistant'. Some dozen years later we know he shared Paul's imprisonment in Rome (Col. 4: 10–12; Philem. 24).

But Mark is also linked in history with Peter. In his first letter (written from Rome) Peter sends greetings to his readers from 'my son Mark'; and, according to an early Christian named Papias, many of the stories about Jesus which Mark records in his Gospel he got from Peter. For such stories Peter was not Mark's only source; but we shall not go far astray if we regard Mark's Gospel as the Story of Jesus as told to John Mark by his friend Peter. It has sixteen chapters which we may divide into four parts.

(1) First comes the Prologue covering the first thirteen verses of chapter 1. In fulfilment of what was said by the Old Testament prophets, John the Baptist appears in the desert country down near the Dead Sea, calling Israel to 'repent', i.e. to return to God, and promising the advent of a much mightier One than himself, viz. the Messiah, or long-expected Saviour. Among those who flock to John's baptism in Jordan comes a young man called Jesus from Nazareth. As he rises streaming from Jordan, all heaven seems to open upon him. A Divine voice tells him he is God's Son and called to be his Messiah. At once Jesus retires into the desert where he is tempted by the devil to turn aside from his God-appointed destiny. So ends the Prologue.

(2) Then, at chapter 1, verse 14, begins the Gospel's first main section, describing the Galilean Ministry. After

the Baptist's arrest by Herod, Jesus comes into Galilee with the startling announcement that the decisive hour of history has struck, and that God's promised Rule, or salvation, is dawning. 'The time is come,' he says, 'the Kingdom of God is upon you. Turn back to God and accept his Good News' (Mark 1: 15).

Jesus now proceeds to call two pairs of brothers from their fishing-nets to become his disciples: 'I will turn you into fishers for men', is his promise. Then, entering the town of Capernaum on the lake-side, he begins to proclaim God's dawning Kingdom both by word and deed. Through all Galilee his fame spreads like a kindling fire. But his claim to forgive sins (a thing that only God was thought able to do), his hob-nobbing with the social outcasts, and his radiant religion shock the Jewish churchmen of the time; and, by and by, he is forced to quit the synagogues (where he had been preaching) and to teach and heal his growing mass of followers by the lake-side.

Twelve men, the nucleus of the Church that is to be, he now appoints to serve him as his lieutenants in the work of the Kingdom. His enemies accuse him of being in league with the devil; others declare him mad. So the Galilean Ministry goes forward, as he teaches the multitudes in parables about God's dawning Reign, and manifests its presence by the mighty works he does.

The Twelve, having been to school with Jesus, are now sent forth, two by two, to tell men the Good News of God's dawning Reign, and to gather God's people. When they return from their mission, the Galilean Ministry culminates in a great mass — feeding near the north end of the lake. So excited are many of his five thousand followers that they see in Jesus what they had been longing for: a King to slay their foes and lead them to victory against hated

Rome.[1] Not such is the destiny ordained for Jesus by his heavenly Father. So, to avoid the dangerous enthusiasm of his supporters, Jesus now leads his little band of twelve north-westwards near the coastal lands of Tyre and Sidon; and on their return journey, at Caesarea Philippi, in the shadow of snow-capped Hermon, a decisive stage in Jesus' Ministry is reached. For Peter, in answer to his Master's question, 'Who do you say I am?' confesses Jesus to be the Messiah, the long-expected Saviour. At once Jesus tells them that, if he is the Messiah, he is a Messiah who must go to his triumph by way of a cross. The disciples are shocked and incredulous; and from that time on the shadow of Calvary falls ever more darkly across the story.

(3) The second main section of the Gospel, covering chapters 9-16, carries the story of Jesus down to the Cross and its tremendous sequel. A week after Peter's confession, Jesus is transfigured — enveloped with an unearthly radiance — on the top of a mountain (probably Hermon), and the disciples receive a heavenly assurance that he is indeed God's Messiah Son who must suffer in order to save. Henceforward the whole story moves towards Jerusalem where Jesus goes, in his own words, 'to give his life as a ransom for many' (10: 45).

Through Galilee to Capernaum they journey, and then travel southwards till they reach Jericho. From Jericho, across Jordan they proceed to Bethany, two miles from Jerusalem.

There follow all the events associated with Holy Week: the Palm Sunday entry into Jerusalem, the temple-cleansing, the priests' plot, the betrayal by Judas. Finally,

[1] See John 6: 14f. which makes explicit what is implied in Mark's picture of 5000 men drawn up in quasi-military formation.

on the Thursday evening, Jesus holds the Last Supper, endures the agony in Gethsemane, is arrested, tried and condemned by Pilate to crucifixion. On the Friday morning at 9 am, he is lifted up on the Cross. At 3 pm, uttering a loud cry, he dies. A few hours later a secret disciple, Joseph of Arimathea, buries his body decently in a rock tomb. It is Friday evening, and, to all human seeming, the story of Jesus is over. . . .

But no! There is a most astounding sequel. On the Sunday morning some women going to the tomb to anoint their Master's body, find it empty, and a mysterious 'young man' tells them: 'He is not here. He is risen. Go, tell his disciples and Peter that he goes before you into Galilee.' Stricken with holy terror, the women flee from the gaping grave . . . (16: 8).

(4) At this point Mark's Gospel ends, its last leaf having been lost. (In the opinion of good scholars the substance of Mark's lost ending is to be found in John 21.) The epilogue, Mark 16: 9–20, is by a later hand. It tells how the risen Lord appeared again to his own and commanded them to preach the Good News to the world.

The Ministry of Jesus which Romans and Jews had done their best to stop was not finished. They had killed Jesus, but destroyed him they had not. On the contrary, he had been 'let loose in the world where neither Roman nor Jew could stop his truth'. The Ministry was going on.

Such is Mark's Gospel. What are its main features? First, its *vivid style*. You would never call Mark a literary man, but he is one of those people who, though they tear grammar to tatters, can really tell a story. His narrative abounds with graphic little touches, often suggesting Peter's eye-witness. He lets us see Jesus sleeping on a rower's cushion in the fishing boat; taking little children in the crook of his arms; looking with love on a rich young man who, refusing his challenge, goes away with a lowering look on his face; or striding on ahead of his disciples, a great lonely figure, on that last journey to Jerusalem.

Next, we are impressed by Mark's *realism*. For him, the Gospel is 'no divine charade'; Jesus is a real man: one who is bone of our bone, flesh of our flesh; now happy, now sad; now very pitiful, now very stern; never blind to the evil in man's heart yet ever gentle with the ignorant and outcast; swift to rebuke all canting hypocrisy yet ever believing that 'with God all things are possible'. In short, Jesus is a genuine man, like us in all respects save sin: so that, as we read his story, we say with Pilate of old (though in another sense) 'Behold the Man!'

But if we stopped there, we should have told only half of Mark's truth about Jesus. Once, centuries later, when an admirer put the name of Kant the great philosopher too near that of Jesus, Kant was horrified. 'He is holy,' he said, 'I'm only a poor bungler doing my best to interpret him.' Mark might have said the same. If for him Jesus is a real man, just as certainly he comes from God, is indeed God's only Son. Read Mark's Gospel carefully and you will find that through it runs *a mysterious undercurrent*. There is something eerie, uncanny, not-of-this-world about Jesus which leaves the crowds in his presence 'amazed' 'astonished' 'awe-struck'. He speaks with a superhuman authority. He possesses powers not given to other men. He is conscious that he is doing a work which only one who is in a true sense divine can do. When therefore we read that the grave could not hold him, we feel that this is the only fit climax to his story. Somehow God is not only *with* this man, but *in* him, so that death has no power over him.

For the story which Mark tells is not of 'one more unfortunate gone to his death', nor yet of one more prophet sealing his testimony to the truth with his life's blood. It is the story of how God's Kingdom, his saving Rule, was once for all manifested in his only Son Jesus who died that the Kingdom might come 'with power' and was raised by God that it might 'be opened to all believers'.

Matthew's Gospel is more comprehensive, Luke's more beautiful, John's more profound. But for the earliest and simplest record of the strong Son of God who (as the Prayer Book says) 'was manifested that he might destroy the works of the devil and make us heirs of eternal life', there is but one book, and its writer lives in history as —

> 'The saint who first found grace to pen
> The life which was the life of men.'

FOR DISCUSSION

1. Why *twelve* apostles?

2. According to Mark, Jesus was both human and divine. Why is it important to maintain the real humanity of Jesus?

4. The Loveliest Gospel (Luke)

From the earliest Gospel we turn now to the third one in our New Testament. If Mark brings to the Story of Jesus realism, and John (as we shall see) depth, Luke's gift is beauty, so that some have accounted it the loveliest book ever written. Later, we shall single out some of the things which have earned it this praise. Meantime, we must deal with the basic introductory questions.

I

The first point to seize is that Luke's Gospel is really Part One of a two-volume work. Part Two is the Acts of the Apostles. In our New Testament St John's Gospel separates the two books; but they belong together just as truly as, say, Stevenson's *Kidnapped* and *Catriona*. If St Luke were writing today, his work would probably bear some such title as this: *The Beginnings of Christianity*, by Dr Luke, in two volumes. Vol. I: How the Good News began with Jesus in Galilee and Jerusalem. Vol. II: How the Apostles brought the Good News from Jerusalem to Rome.

But what proof have we that Luke was the author? First, if you compare the Prefaces to the Gospel and to Acts and study the style of the two books generally, you must conclude that the same hand wrote both. Next, in Acts, chapters 16–28, we come on certain passages (Acts 16: 10–17; 20: 5–21: 18; 27: 1–28: 16) where the writer suddenly lapses into the first person plural, saying 'we' where elsewhere he says 'they'. These 'We passages', as they are called, which read like extracts from his travel diary, show that the writer had travelled a good deal with St Paul, and went with him finally to Rome. Now among those who were with the apostle in Rome was 'Luke the beloved physician' (Col. 4: 14, Philem. 24).

This argument about the Gospel's authorship which has begun to point in Luke's direction is confirmed (*a*) by the presence here and there in the Gospel and Acts of what sounds like medical phraseology (Luke 4: 38, 8: 43; Acts 9: 18, 28: 8) and (*b*) by the tradition of the Church in the second century. This unanimously named Luke as the author. There is a strong presumption that the tradition is right. Had the Gospel's authorship been unknown and they had been casting about for an author's name, the odds are that they would have picked on an apostle and not on a comparatively unknown person like Luke.

What then do we know about Doctor Luke? There are three New Testament references to him. To Col. 4: 14 and Philem. 24, already mentioned, we have to add 2 Tim. 4: 11. Besides these we have a number of traditions about him, the likeliest of which says he was a native of Antioch.

What these tell us is that Luke was a Gentile by birth (cf. Col. 4: 10–14), a physician by profession, a Christian by conversion, and a friend of Paul's by choice. For the rest, if you wish to know what manner of man he was, the answer is: 'By his books you shall know him.'

They reveal a man of generous and gentle instincts, far more cultured than Mark, and yet, so far from being a 'highbrow', a man of quick human sympathies, loving his Lord not least because he had been ever 'the friend of publicans and sinners'.

Tradition says that Luke wrote his Gospel in Greece, probably about AD 75. How and why did he come to write it? For the answer we turn to the Preface to his Gospel:

'Inasmuch as many have undertaken to complete a narrative of the things which have been accomplished among us, just as they were delivered to us by those who from the beginning were eye-witnesses and ministers of the word, it seemed good to me also, having followed all things closely for some time past, to write an orderly account for you, most excellent Theophilus, that you may know the truth concerning the things of which you have been informed' (Luke 1: 1–4. RSV).

Luke, then, wrote in order to give 'his Excellency Theophilus' a reliable account of Christ's life and teaching. We do not know who precisely Theophilus was, but he was obviously a man of high social rank. ('Right Honourable' would be our modern mode of address to him.) No doubt Theophilus was typical of the sort of readers Luke had in his mind when he wrote. If this is so, we may say that he planned a Story of Christ better calculated to appeal to educated men like Theophilus than the rather roughly-written Gospel of Mark, an account too which would make it clearer than Mark does that Jesus was not only the Messiah of the Jews but the Saviour of all men.

The other point worth noting in that Preface of Luke's is his claim that, before taking up his pen, he had 'gone into the available sources', as we would say. Thanks to modern scholars we can make a pretty good guess at what they were. One of them was the Gospel of Mark. Another was a collection of Jesus' sayings which the scholars call 'Q' (from the German *Quelle* 'source'). But Luke had also much new material about Jesus which he had himself gathered, probably during the two years he was at Caesarea in the company of Paul (AD 57–59). To these we must add the stories relating to Jesus' birth, probably derived from the Christians in Judea.

It is with these stories of the Bethlehem birth, which have inspired so many of our Christmas carols, that he begins his Gospel (1–2). Next come the Baptism and Temptation of Jesus (3: 1–4, 13). Then follow the record of the Ministry in Galilee (4: 14–9: 50) and the account of his journey to Jerusalem (9: 51–19: 10). In this last section occur most of the narratives and parables which we specially associate with the name of Luke. Finally, he tells the story of the Cross and the Resurrection, narrating new facts and details about the Passion and the appearances of the risen Lord (19: 11–24: 53).

II

So much by way of summarizing the Gospel. Now we must pick out some of the features which go to make it, as Renan said, 'the most beautiful book in the world'.

There is a tradition that Luke was an artist in his spare time. Whether or not he was a painter, he was certainly an artist in words, and the beauty of his style comes through even in translation; not a word too many, and each chosen perfectly for its purpose. Out of many examples take two. Where in all literature will you find a story better told than that of the Father and his two sons (Luke 15)? So fine a word-master as Robert Bridges pronounced it 'an absolutely flawless piece of work'. The other example is the tale of the Walk to Emmaus (Luke 24). Not only is that encounter with the risen Christ narrated to perfection, but, as Malcolm Muggeridge has said, 'There is something in the very language and manner of it which breathes truth.'

Style is a wonderful gift, but it is not Luke's skill as a writer alone which has earned his Gospel universal esteem. What he has to say about Jesus is as notable as how he tells it.

Some years ago there appeared a book by A. E. Whitham with the title *The Catholic Christ*, the adjective being used of course without ecclesiastical connotation. This is the Christ Luke gives us. If in Matthew Jesus is the Messianic King foretold in prophecy, and in Mark the Man who is also the strong Son of God, in Luke we are shown Jesus the Saviour of men. Luke traces back his genealogy not merely to Abraham (as Matthew does) but to Adam; he shows us Simeon hailing the infant Jesus as 'a light to lighten the Gentiles'; he singles out a Roman centurion for the highest praise, 'I have not found so great faith, no, not in Israel'; and he ends his Gospel with a command of the risen Lord to preach the Gospel 'to all nations'.

Next, observe how Luke highlights Christ's concern for the underdogs of society, for the last, the least and the lost. Thus he relates how Jesus forgave a woman of the streets when his host, a pious Pharisee, would have shown her the door; he tells how Jesus made a new man of that hated inspector of taxes, Zaccheus of Jericho; he records how the dying Lord promised paradise to a thief who hung beside him on Calvary. And as Luke ever shows a lively sympathy for the poor and outcast, so he holds up for rebuke the loveless rich, like Dives in the parable.

Were Luke publishing his Gospel today, I suspect the reviewers would style him 'an ardent feminist'. Again and

c

again he goes out of his way to show us the tender chivalry of Christ to women, or the part they played in his ministry. Women figure prominently in the Birth Stories: Elisabeth, mother of John the Baptist; Anna, the aged prophetess who gave thanks for the wonderful Child; and of course 'Mary his mother'. But these are only the first of many: women like the Widow of Nain, Mary Magdalene and Joanna, the wife of Herod's steward, the two sisters Martha and Mary from Bethany, not to mention the 'daughters of Jerusalem' who wept for Jesus on the way to the Cross, or the faithful three who, on the first Easter morning, went early with spices to anoint Jesus' body, only to find the tomb empty.

The other evangelists tell us that it was Jesus' habit to go apart and, in communion with his heavenly Father, seek to discover his will for him. But more than any other Luke shows us 'the kneeling Christ', praying before his Baptism in Jordan, praying before his Transfiguration on the Mount, praying in the Garden of Gethsemane, praying on the Cross. It was the same interest that led Luke to preserve and record three of Christ's finest parables about Prayer: the Pharisee and the Publican, the Importunate Widow, and the Friend at Midnight.

Artistry in word-painting, catholicity in his portrait of Christ, a constant concern to depict our Lord as the champion of the outcast, the friend of women and a true man of prayer . . . yet there is one more feature in Luke's Gospel which helps to give it its perennial appeal.

Luke's is the *Gospel of joy*. There is gladness in its beginning: 'Behold, I bring you glad tidings of great joy' (2: 10). There is gladness in the middle, a whole chapter of it, in parables — Lost Sheep, Lost Coin, Lost Son (15).

And there is gladness at its ending when, after the risen Christ had parted from his disciples, they 'returned to Jerusalem with great joy' (24: 52).

Small wonder that Luke's Gospel remains the favourite Gospel of many folk today. His is the kind of book which brings health to the soul in an age like ours. Its author is still a physician and still beloved.

FOR DISCUSSION

1. How much the poorer would have been our knowledge of the life, character and teaching of Jesus if Luke had not written his Gospel?

2. Three of Jesus' seven sayings from the Cross occur only in Luke's Gospel. What are they?

5. The Profoundest Gospel (John)

The Gospel of John, which was the favourite of such very different men as John Knox and William Wordsworth, has long been the text-book of the parish minister and the inspiration of the straight-forward layman. Still to this day, by common consent, words from it have a wonderful power to comfort us in times of bereavement or calamity. Why should this be so? The short answer is: because to a wonderful simplicity St John adds a divine depth in telling the Story of Stories. 'Never in my life,' testified Luther, 'have I read a book written in simpler words, and yet the words are inexpressible.' Here is set forth the eternal meaning of what God did when he spoke to us through his Son and gave him for our salvation.

I

Who wrote this Gospel, where, when and why? These are questions which have much exercised the scholars and cannot be discussed at length now. I can only give you my own view, reached after long years of study.

The Gospel was written in Ephesus between AD 70 and 80 by a man called John the Elder. This John was a close disciple of John the apostle who lived the latter part of his life in Ephesus. John the apostle is not only 'the beloved disciple' mentioned five times in the Gospel, but he is *the authority* behind it. Study of the Gospel suggests that the apostle was a man of special insight and that Jesus meant him to be the particular guardian of his revelation (see John 20: 8, 21: 7, 24), and such he became by the Gospel which embodies his testimony. Why was the Gospel written? The answer is in the last verse of chapter 20: 'These things are written that you may believe that Jesus is the Christ the Son of God, and that believing you may have life in his name.'

'Life', or, in its fuller form, 'eternal life' (for there is no difference of meaning) is the key-word of this Gospel. By 'eternal life' is meant life which is life indeed, life of a new quality, life of which Jesus is the mediator (10: 10), life which begins here and now (17: 3), life which, because it is God's own life, can never die.

What readers had John in view when he wrote? Since 'all religion is a prayer for life' (Sabatier), the answer is: all people interested in new life, Jews and Greeks, Christians and non-Christians.

In origin, let us remember, the Gospel had dealt in Jewish concepts like 'the Kingdom of God' and 'the Messiah'. When, however, John wrote, the Church numbered more Gentiles than Jews, and to them these Jewish concepts did not mean so much. They were posing other questions. What place did Jesus hold in God's saving purpose for men? What was the chief blessing the Gospel offered? How did Jesus remain a living force among men? Such were the questions John answered in his Gospel. Jesus, he said, is the saving Word, or Purpose, of God in human terms. The supreme blessing which the Gospel offers is eternal life. And to the question, 'How does Jesus remain a living power in the world?' St John answers: Because he has come back, through the Holy Spirit, to abide with all believers, to remind them of what he had

said, and to guide them into all the truth of the Gospel
(14: 25, 15: 13).

II

All this suggests that John's is *a Gospel with a difference*. This
is evident even in a short analysis of its contents, thus:

   (i) The Coming of God in Christ (1)
   (ii) His Revelation to the world (2–12)
   (iii) His Revelation to the Disciples (13–17)
   (iv) The Conflict of Light with Darkness (18–19)
   (v) The Dawn (20)
   (vi) The Commission of the risen Lord (21).

Darkness and light, judgment and salvation, death and
life — these are the Gospel's main themes.

It begins differently — not at Jordan (Mark) or at
Bethlehem (Matthew and Luke), but in eternity. 'When
all things began, the Word already was' (1: 1 NEB); then
'the Word became flesh' (1: 14). Why? Answer: 'No one
has ever seen God; the only Son who is in the bosom of
the Father, he has made him known' (1: 18). That is, the
Story about to be unfolded is the word 'God' spelt out in
human words and deeds. All that mortal men can take in
about the nature of the unseen God is ours in Jesus Christ.

Though it is basically the same story of Christ's earthly
ministry which the other three evangelists had related,
John tells it with quite a difference. Thus he records a
preliminary ministry of Jesus in Judea before the Galilean
ministry began, and an extended one in Jerusalem after
the Galilean one was over. Some of the stories the other
evangelists had recorded, e.g. the cure of the Officer's Son
and the Feeding of the Five Thousand, John re-tells in his
own way. But, if he omits episodes like the Temptation and
the Transfiguration, John has new stories to relate: the

marriage at Cana, the healing of the Bethesda cripple, the raising of Lazarus, the Washing of the Disciples' Feet, Christ's appearance on the first Easter morning to Mary Magdalene, and a later one to seven disciples by the Lake in the grey of a Galilean dawn.

Again, St John calls Jesus' miracles (of which he records seven) not 'mighty works' but 'signs'. He dates the crucifixion a day earlier than Mark did. He represents the Cross as the place where the world's judgment was enacted and the glory of God supremely revealed, so that his account of the Resurrection (which has all the freshness of dawn on a spring day), is like the quiet rising of the sun which has already vanquished night.

Why these differences? There are at least two reasons. One is that John had at his disposal much early and independent information about Jesus' works and words, relating not only to the course of the Ministry but to his Passion and Resurrection. This new tradition is precious because it clearly goes back to the first decades after the actual events and at point after point illuminates the Story of Jesus as the other evangelists tell it.[1]

The other reason is that John aimed to tell the Story of Jesus *in depth*, to bring out its ultimate meaning. This is why he opens as he does, why he calls the miracles 'signs', i.e. symbolic pointers to what and who Jesus is, and why he portrays the Passion and the Resurrection as he does.

The other evangelists had not of course been blind to the eternal meaning John finds in the Story of Jesus. Even in Mark's account of the Baptism, for example, he tries, in oriental imagery, to suggest a traffic between two worlds, the heavenly world breaking into this one. But in Mark these features occur only here and there, like breaks in the

[1] See C. H. Dodd, *Historical Tradition in The Fourth Gospel* (1963).

cloud revealing glimpses of the infinite blue vault beyond. John saw the whole story of Jesus thus. For him it is 'an earthly story' — and he will have no truck with those who deny it — but it is 'an earthly story with a heavenly meaning'. This 'heavenly meaning' is not something superimposed on a plain tale which would be better told without it. It is the true meaning of the blessed thing God did when he sent Jesus. And the proof of this is that John's Gospel does make full sense of the other Gospels and is in fact, as Calvin said, the key which unlocks their secrets.

III

Now, finally, let us try to answer the question 'Wherein resides the perennial appeal of John's Gospel of which we spoke at the beginning?'.

First, as we have said, in its new historical light on Jesus. Not so long ago, when some men set out to tell the Story of Jesus, they had a way of dismissing this Gospel as theology without any rootage in real history. Recent research shows that this is no longer a tenable position, that the Gospel rests back on early Palestinian tradition which can be used to amplify and illuminate the earlier Gospels.

Second, the words which Robert Browning sets on the lips of the dying apostle John (in his 'A Death in the Desert') are profoundly true:

'What first were guessed as points I now knew stars
And named them in the Gospel I have writ.'

John's great achievement was to take the Gospel 'points' and set them forth in their starry glory. For example, in Mark Jesus' use of 'Father' as a name for God occurs four times; in John the figure is 107. Or take Jesus' own awareness of being the unique Son of God. In the earlier Gospels this is stated, or implied, about half a dozen times. In John's Gospel it is an ever-recurring theme. Or yet again, recall how, quite briefly, in the first three Gospels Jesus promises his disciples that they will have the Holy Spirit to help them in time of need. In John that promise is spelt out, with rich detail, in the five 'Paraclete' Sayings found in chapters 14–16. This 'Paraclete' (or 'Stand-by' as we may translate it), viz. the Holy Spirit will come (says Jesus) not so much to supply his absence as to accomplish his presence and serve them as Remembrancer, Guide, Strengthener and Friend.

Third, John not only gives us the Gospel of eternal life, but in it he presents the challenge of Jesus, who brings it, in what nowadays we would call an 'existential' way. (Existential thinking is the sort a man does when he feels that his whole existence is at stake. It is the kind a man does when as lover he declares his passion, as a statesman he commits his country to war, or when on his deathbed he clings to his faith.)

It is on such existential terms that the Christ of St John calls on men to decide. The alternatives are 'Life *or* Death' — that is, real life, life lived with God here and now, life that can never die; *or* spiritual death, separation from God the fountain of life, 'perishing' for ever from his presence. (See John 3: 16.) A like 'existential' note sounds through Christ's teaching about judgment. Judgment is not simply something that happens at a great end-of-the-world Assize. It is happening *now*, as God is —

> 'sifting out the hearts of men
> Before his judgment seat.'

And men judge themselves by the response which they make to his Christ who is the only 'true and living way' to the unseen Father (John 14: 6):

'He who believes in him is not condemned,
He who does not believe is condemned already,
Because he has not believed in the name of the only Son of God (3: 18).

But the Christ of St John who in 'the days of his flesh' called on men thus to decide, is no mere figure in an old, old story. By the power of the Holy Spirit, he is our eternal Contemporary; and it is not from Palestine only, or the first century, but here and now he is to be heard and encountered. To us he utters the same command as to Philip, 'Follow me!' (1: 43). Still today he challenges the enquirer as he did in Jerusalem: 'If any man will do his will, he will know of the doctrine, whether it is of God' (7: 17). To those who long for life that will never die, he says, 'I am the Resurrection and the Life . . . Because I live you will live also' (11: 25, 14: 18). And now, as of old to his disciples, he promises: 'Peace I leave with you; my peace I give unto you. Not as the world giveth, give I unto you. Let not your heart be troubled, neither let it be afraid' (14: 27).

FOR DISCUSSION

1. Some people are put off or puzzled by the 'philosophy' at the beginning of John's Gospel (1: 1–18). Why do you think John began this way?

2. John 3: 16 has been called 'the Gospel within the Gospels' and the greatest verse in the New Testament. Do you agree?

6. How they brought the Good News from Jerusalem to Rome (Acts)

It is time now to turn from the Gospels to the Acts of the Apostles which is *the bridge* between them and the rest of the New Testament.

Some of you may remember Browning's thrilling ballad, 'How they brought the Good News from Ghent to Aix.' Change the two place-names and for Ghent and Aix write Jerusalem and Rome, and you have a perfect description of Acts. It is the story of how the apostles, or special messengers, of Christ brought his Good News from the Holy City to the Capital of the world. And what a stirring tale it is, this of how the Church began, moved outwards, broke down barriers, and spread all over the known world! Here are travels and adventures in plenty — plots and escapes, earthquakes and shipwrecks, trials and prisons, riots and victories, with all the sights and sounds of the Middle East in the first century of our era — Palestine, Syria, Galatia, Asia, Greece, Cyprus, Malta, Rome. And all in the course of three crucial decades, AD 30–60.

I

The writer of this book was the author of the Third Gospel, Luke, 'the beloved physician' as Paul called him (Col. 4: 14). Acts, as we saw earlier, is really Volume Two of his work on the beginnings of Christianity. Volume One had related 'all that Jesus began to do and to teach'

(Acts 1: 1). But Jesus had promised 'The works that I do shall you do also', and in Volume Two Dr Luke tells how the promise came true: how the apostles, inspired by the Holy Spirit, took the Good News from Palestine across the blue Mediterranean to Corinth, Athens and eventually to the metropolis of the ancient world.

Both his books Dr Luke dedicated to 'his excellency Theophilus' who, as we observed earlier, was obviously a man of high rank and some culture. Doubtless Theophilus typified the kind of readers Luke wished to reach with his writing. When he composed his work — probably about AD 75–80 — many slanderous stories were circulating about the Christians. So Luke set himself to give Theophilus and his like a reliable account of the new religion and to vindicate its fair name in the eyes of his Gentile readers. In particular, he sought to show that Christianity presented no threat to Rome and the *Pax Romana*, as its enemies were wickedly insinuating.

What sources had Luke at his disposal when he composed the Acts of the Apostles? In the second half of his book which deals with Paul and his friends, we need not doubt his sources of information. He possessed his own travel diary of which the 'we passages' are extracts (see p. 22), and of course he had Paul himself. But in the first half of his book, where he is recording events which happened before he himself came on the scene, he had to rely on what others told him. Thus for his account of the Mother Church in Jerusalem he probably depended on Mark and Peter. Philip the evangelist who lived in the port of Caesarea and whom Luke knew personally (Acts 21: 8f.), must be his source for what he tells us about that city. As for the church at Antioch, he knew many Christians there, and he may even himself have been an Antiochene.

II

The twenty-eight chapters of the book of Acts (which make it the longest in the New Testament) cover a period of thirty years — from AD 30 to AD 60, from the Resurrection of Jesus to Paul's arrival in Rome.

We may conveniently divide it into two parts. Part One (chapters 1 to 12), tells how Peter and the first Christians brought the Gospel from Jerusalem to Antioch in Syria, the third greatest city in the Roman empire, and the place where the name 'Christian' was first coined.

Here, after an opening chapter which describes Jesus' leave-taking of the disciples and the election of Matthias to fill the place of the traitor Judas, we get a glimpse of the young church in Jerusalem on the day of Pentecost when the promised Holy Spirit came upon the disciples, and of the spread of the Gospel in and around Jerusalem. Under the impulsion of the Spirit the Church grows apace, with Peter as its undisputed leader. At first there is no open breach with Jewry; but by and by the new wine of the Gospel begins to burst the old wineskins. Stephen, the first to grasp the essential newness of Christianity, calls down on himself the wrath of the Jews and is stoned to death. At once persecution breaks out, and with the consequent scattering of Christians the circle of the Gospel's influence widens, and the hallowed fire spreads to Samaria, to Caesarea and then to Antioch destined to become the cradle of Gentile Christianity.

Part Two consists of chapters 13 to 28. If in Part One Peter was the key figure, it is now Paul who leads the advance from Antioch to Rome. First we see him with Barnabas setting out on a pioneering mission to Cyprus (of which Barnabas was a native) and then crossing the sea to Galatia in Asia Minor (modern Turkey). After this follows the first Council of the Church in Jerusalem to decide on what terms Gentiles are to be admitted into the Christian fellowship, an issue brought to a head by the missionary success of Paul and Barnabas. Then Paul, this time with Silas, makes a second journey in the course of which, after revisiting Asia Minor, they bring the Gospel to Europe, and in Macedonia, Athens and Corinth the Faith is proclaimed.

Paul's third journey sees the Gospel firmly planted in the great heathen city of Ephesus before he once again sets foot in Europe.

Then in his last nine chapters (20–28) Dr Luke's history moves to its climax. Returning to Jerusalem, Paul is attacked by the unbelieving Jews, and for his own safety put under arrest by the Romans. As a Roman citizen he appeals to Caesar for justice. For two years he lies in gaol in Caesarea; then at last he is taken by sea to Rome, being ship-wrecked on Malta en route; and Luke's narrative ends with Paul in his Roman prison awaiting the Emperor's verdict.

'The victory of the Word of God,' says an old scholar, 'Paul at Rome; the culmination of the Gospel, the end of Acts. It began at Jerusalem. It finishes at Rome.' Having described 'the last lap', Luke has completed what he set out to do. He has described the Gospel's 'road to Rome', that sinful City on the Seven Hills (as men called it): Rome, the centre of civilization as Luke knew it, symbol of the world as it is, and of man in need of salvation.

III

Now let us try to evaluate the author and his book. They say that 'the style is the man'. What kind of man and writer does Luke show himself to be in Acts?

First, an *honest man and an accurate reporter*: an honest man because he doesn't pretend that the first Christians were all sinless saints — he lets us hear, for example, a cursing Peter and a quarrelling Paul (8: 20 and 15: 39); and an accurate recorder, because, whether it be the geography of the Mediterranean world in the first century, or the titles of the officials and magistrates in the various cities ('praetors' in Philippi, 'proconsuls' in Corinth, 'politarchs' in Thessalonika), or the procedures and intricacies of Roman law, Luke gets his details right, as scholars of the calibre of Sir William Ramsay, H. J. Cadbury, and Sherwin-Whyte have shown.

Next, if Luke is a reliable reporter, he is no mere dry-as-dust recorder of dead facts. He is *a man who can make history come alive*, whether it be the heroic martyrdom of Stephen; Peter's preaching at Caesarea; Paul and Silas with their feet in the stocks at Philippi and still able to sing hymns; the tremendous riot in the theatre at Ephesus with the crowd, roused to fury, shouting 'Great is Diana of the Ephesians!'; that terrific storm and shipwreck on Paul's voyage to Rome. And with what life-like figures Luke packs his pages: Peter now much more like a 'Rock' than when Jesus first gave him the nickname; Paul the dauntless; that fine Christian couple, Priscilla and Aquila (with, as we guess, 'the grey mare the better horse'); good-hearted Barnabas; eloquent Apollos. Not to mention the notable Jews and Gentiles who come within the orbit of the advancing Gospel: Gamaliel the rabbi, Simon the Sorcerer, Demetrius the silversmith of Ephesus (with his fellow trade-unionists), the Roman proconsul Gallio of Corinth who turned away his dainty nose lest the breath of the Ghetto should come between him and his nobility.

Finally, though Luke was a historian — the Church's

first one — he was, in his own way, *an evangelist*. Setting out to write history, he nonetheless used his historical data to preach the Gospel of redemption through Christ. Luke was in fact the first of a long line of doctors who have seen in Jesus God's 'good physician' to sin-sick men, and who viewed this world through Christian eyes. The theology of salvation which Luke proclaims as he tells his story is centred in Christ the risen and exalted Lord in whose name men are offered the forgiveness of sins and new life, and the power by which this comes to pass is the Holy Spirit who so dominates Luke's second volume that it has been called 'the Book of the Holy Spirit'.

Our debt to Luke can hardly be over-rated. Without his book how little we should know of the events immediately following the Resurrection, how ignorant we should be of the events which led to the writing of the New Testament epistles! Acts is the link which binds together the Gospels and the rest of the New Testament.

But there is another side to its importance. For many the value of the book is that it forms a bridge between the days of Christ's ministry and ourselves. There are always people who think that believing in Christ today is harder for us than for those who knew him during his earthly life. Their unspoken cry is, 'O had I lived in that great day!' But they are wrong. This nostalgic longing for a figure in past history is not Christianity. We worship not a dead hero but a living Lord. Right from the beginning the Christians never thought primarily of Christ as a person in past history; they had no wish to turn back the clock and re-live the dear dead days in Galilee. For them the paramount miracle was not Jesus, a great good man of yester year, but Christ the Lord, present now with them through the Holy Spirit's power. Following Christ meant not the endeavour to imitate the moral stature of the man Jesus but living in a quite new fellowship — the company of those in whom the living Christ moved and worked.

Thus Acts helps us to a true view of what Christianity is. For in it we see men and women who, though Christ's bodily presence is no longer with them, know that he lives and reigns and that, through the Holy Spirit, his help is available for them in all the changing scenes of life.

FOR DISCUSSION

1. A good church historian should get his facts right, possess a lively style, and be able to discern the hand of God in the movement of events. How far does Dr Luke in Acts measure up to these requirements?

2. Again and again in Acts Luke finds the secret of the Church's victorious advance in the leading of the Holy Spirit. Does the hope of revival in the Church today lie, as the Neo-Pentecostalists say, in a rediscovery of the reality and power of the Spirit?

7. The Most Important Letter ever written (Romans)

In our study of Acts we saw how much Paul did to spread the Gospel in the world. But he was no less great as a theologian and an administrator; and the New Testament has preserved many of those letters he wrote to the churches about the nature and truth of Christianity. Three of these we shall study. We shall start with the greatest one, Romans; then consider the smallest one, that to Philemon; and end with what may have been Paul's last one, Philippians.

First, then, Paul's magnum opus, Romans. Martin Luther called it 'the chief book in the New Testament and the purest Gospel'. S. T. Coleridge pronounced it 'the most profound work in existence'. And a modern American professor with the good Scottish name of John Knox declares it 'unquestionably the most important letter ever written'.

You may think these verdicts a bit overdone. Yet when you recall the immense influence this letter has had on men's thinking down nineteen centuries, its right to be called the most important letter ever written does not seem ill founded. In practically every great revival in the Christian Church, and in every theological re-awakening, Romans has played a key part. Nor is its day done, and we may safely prophesy that so long as Christianity lasts, this letter written more than nineteen hundred years ago in a back street of Corinth will take men back to the living heart of the Gospel.

Why should Romans be so important? Because in this letter written about AD 57 in Corinth during Paul's third missionary journey, we have the answer to the question 'What is Christianity?' by the greatest thinker in the early Church. Paul wrote *urbi* — to the city called Rome; but, without knowing it, he wrote *orbi* — to the world; and what he wrote for his own time has been found to be written for all time.

It would be impertinent of me to suggest that in a few pages I could lay bare all the spiritual riches of Romans. What I can do is to analyze the contents of the letter and give you a clear idea of its message and its relevance for the world today.

Romans has sixteen chapters. The last one, which is mostly a list of names, we can omit now. For our purpose we may also pass fairly quickly over chapters 9–11, a part of the letter Paul may have composed separately, at an earlier date. In these three chapters he faces the question over which, as a Jew, he had long agonized: 'Why have the Jews, God's chosen people, rejected their Messiah and apparently excluded themselves from the grace of God?'

First (chapter 9), he surveys the problem from the Divine side, saying, 'God is sovereign Lord of history and may do as he wills.' Second (10), he considers the problem from the human side, and says, 'The Jews have excluded themselves by their own faithlessness and by going the wrong way about finding salvation.' But he cannot rest in this sad conclusion, and in his final word on the subject (11) he says, 'Just as the Gentiles, once disobedient, have found God's mercy, so it will be with the Jews. Universal disobedience is to issue in universal salvation.'

Now let us focus on chapters 1–8 and 12–15 which contain the heart of the letter.

Paul starts with a greeting to the Christians in Rome, and follows it with a thanksgiving in which he tells them that his letter is meant to pave the way for his long-intended visit to Rome. (He did reach Rome, we may recall, but in chains.) Rome needs the Gospel, he says, for it is God's power for saving sinners, and Rome has no lack of these.

From this point (1: 17) on, you can divide his argument up into three parts:

(1) 1: 17–3: 20   The Sin of Man
(2) 3: 21–8: 39   But the Grace of God
(3) 12: 1–15: 13   Therefore the Christian Ethic.

In the Gospel, Paul begins, 'the righteousness of God is revealed'. Here is one of Paul's key-phrases. The NEB rightly renders the Greek 'God's way of righting wrong', for the phrase denotes not a divine attribute, but a divine *activity*. It means 'God putting things right' for his people by rescuing them from their sins or from evil men. Through long centuries Israel had prayed that God would so put things right, that he would intervene decisively in history to 'visit and redeem his people'. Now, Paul says, in the events that make up the Gospel story — in the ministry, death and resurrection of Christ — God is to be seen doing just this.

But why is the righteousness of God needed? Because of the *un*righteousness of men. All men — Jews and Gentiles alike — have sinned by breaking God's law. (But, surely, the Gentiles never had a law to break? Yes, they had — God has written on their hearts an intuitive sense of right and wrong. Rom. 2: 14f.) Why, Paul says, you have only to look at pagan society — its worship of false gods issuing in obscene immorality — to see how God's retribution is falling on their sins. Lose the true God, and that is the slough of evil into which you sink. Nor are the Jews one whit better. God has revealed his will to them in the law of Moses — the Ten Commandments and the rest — and they have consistently flouted it. Thus all men, without exception, are guilty at the bar of God, as the scriptures say.

Such is the disease. Now, at 3: 21, Paul turns to the Divine remedy. After long forbearance with men's sins God has begun to put things right. In Christ he has provided a way for guilty men to be 'justified' — to get right with God. For by works of law — by his own moral achievements — no mortal man can put himself right with God.

Here then begins the record of God's grace — his extravagant goodness — to sinful men. God has made the Cross his 'mercy seat', the place of his forgiveness. When sinners by faith commit themselves to Christ who, by God's appointing, has died for their sins, God pardons them and sets them in a new relationship with himself.

Is this 'justification by faith' something new? On the contrary it is as old as Genesis and Abraham, the man who, by taking God at his word, found acceptance with him. 'Abram put his faith in the Lord,' we read (Gen. 15: 6), 'and the Lord counted that faith to him for righteousness.' Just so, Christian faith means taking God at his living word in Christ — the Christ who died and rose for our saving (4).

Being justified by God's grace through faith, what do we gain? Peace with God which makes our suffering take on new meaning and leads us to rely to the uttermost on the love which went to the Cross to deliver us. As from Adam came sin and death for his descendants, so from the second Adam come righteousness and new life for all who trust in him (5).

This new life means, first, deliverance from the dominion
of *sin*. This is symbolized in baptism which admits us into
God's people, the Church. There, in union with Christ,
we die to our old bad life and rise into a new righteous one,
and we are called to become what we now potentially are
— men dead to sin and alive to God (6).

Next, it means deliverance from *the Law* and the deadly
grip it can lay on us through the power of sin in 'the flesh',
i.e. our lower nature. Not in itself evil, the Law yet makes
a man conscious of sin and provokes him to sinning. Once,
Paul says, I too lived under the Law. The good I wanted
to do I could not, and the evil that I would not that I did.
So I was reduced to complete despair till God delivered me
through Christ (7).

Finally, for those united with Christ there is deliverance
from Divine *condemnation*. What the Law could not do —
break the hold sin has on us through our lower nature —
God has done in another way, through Christ and the
Cross.

Now, as a result, not only are our sins forgiven, but we
have God's life-giving Spirit energizing in us, aiding us in
our prayers, making us cry 'Abba Father', shaping us to
the likeness of God's Son, and — if we are ready to suffer
with him — assuring us that we are fellow-heirs with
Christ of his immortal life. Trials and tribulations may
now be our portion but they are not to be compared with
the glory God has in store for us. We are more than
conquerors through him that loved us, and nothing in this
world or out of it shall be able to separate us from the love
of God in Christ (8).

But if the Gospel has a believing side, no less has it a
behaving side. So in chapter 12 Paul outlines the Christian
Ethic and discusses the conduct befitting men who have

experienced God's grace. It is a life lived 'in Christ', i.e. one lived in the community of which he is the living Head, so that it can be called his Body. And it is a life characterized by *agapé* — that self-spending love described so memorably in 1 Cor. 13.

Christian morality, Paul begins, is our response to God's mercy in Christ. As members of his Body, each has his own gift to be used for the good of all. Make your love genuine, be aglow with the Spirit, persist in prayer, be open-handed to the needy. Bless your persecutors. Repay no one evil for evil. Live peaceably with all men. Overcome evil with good (12) (Observe how reminiscent this is of the Sermon on the Mount. In chapters 12–14 there are at least nine echoes of Christ's moral teaching.)

In chapter 13 Paul's theme is the Christian's attitude to the State. As Christians, he says, we must be law-abiding citizens, recognizing that the civil powers are ordained of God, as we must pay all lawful dues and taxes. One debt only the Christian never may discharge — the debt of love. Love your neighbour truly, and you have fulfilled the whole Law.

Then Paul sounds a reveille. God's new day is breaking, he warns, therefore Christians should be children of the dawn, casting off the works of darkness, putting on the armour of light, and arraying themselves in the moral habits of Christ himself (13).

Having outlined the Christian Ethic, Paul, in 14: 1–15: 13, adds a special word on the need for Christian tolerance. If, he says, little rifts appear in your fellowship due to squabbles about meat-eating or observing certain days, the Christian law of love requires that both the 'strong' Christians (those who have no narrow scruples about days or foods) and the 'weak' ones (those who have such scruples) should show tolerance to each other. We are all members of the Saviour's fellowship, and each should respect the other man's conscience. Therefore no judging, one of another. Put no stumbling block in a brother's way. Never for the sake of food destroy the work of God, but pursue the things that make for peace.

In short, imitate Christ who never considered himself. Consult your neighbour's good and aim to build up the Church's common life. Christ has accepted us all. Therefore let us accept each other.

There, in brief, you have Christianity according to St Paul. First, the diagnosis of man's spiritual malaise; then the prescription of God's remedy for it; and finally, the charting of the new way in which the saved man should walk, with the hope of glory at journey's ending.

Nearly two thousand years have elapsed since Paul wrote Romans. We live in quite other times, and under other skies. Since Paul's time the whole face of the world has changed in many ways. Yet I suggest that Paul, being dead, still speaks to our condition today, and that his prescription for our spiritual predicament is the right one.

No one will pretend that with the passage of 1900 years the human heart has changed materially. For all the amazing advances made in science and other fields of human activity, man remains the same sin-sick unhappy proposition that Paul knew, still fondly believing that he can save himself by some device or effort of his own — by higher education, improved psychological techniques, or political restructuring — only to be sadly disillusioned again and again, because —

> 'The heart ay's the part aye
> That makes us right or wrang'

and it is there, within us, that, as Jesus said (Mark 7: 20–23), the root of the trouble lies.

Not so very long ago many people had relegated Paul's teaching about original sin to the rag-bag of outmoded superstitions, holding that man was innately good and his civilization advancing irresistibly to perfection. We know better now. 'To judge by the facts,' wrote the late Richard Crossman, 'there is a great deal more to be said for the Christian doctrine of original sin than for Rousseau's theory of the noble savage or Marx's of the classless society.' By the two colossal human disasters of this century and their awful aftermaths still with us, we have been taught in blood and tears how dread a laboratory of good and evil is the heart of man. In the event Paul emerges as a better diagnostician of our human situation than all the H. G. Wellses of our time. Evil is real, is something radical, racial and endemic in mankind for which the Gospel of God's redeeming grace in Christ alone provides the cure.

Of course all this remains absurd to the humanists of today as it was 'foolishness' to the ancient Greeks. But to us who are Christians 'the foolishness of God' is, as Paul said to the Corinthians, 'wiser than men' (1 Cor. 1: 25); and with the apostle we say, 'I am not ashamed of the Gospel, for it is the power of God for salvation to every man who has faith.' (Rom. 1: 16).

FOR DISCUSSION

1. Why do modern Christians seldom read St Paul?

2. 'In the New Testament religion is grace and ethics is gratitude' (Erskine of Linlathen). How does Romans illustrate this truth?

8. The Most Gentlemanly Letter ever written (Philemon)

From Romans, Paul's greatest letter, we turn to his smallest, that to Philemon.

The finest comment on it was made by John Duncan, a famous professor of Hebrew in Edinburgh, affectionately known to his students as 'Rabbi' Duncan. He called it 'the most gentlemanly letter ever written'. Let us see why.

I am not going to bother you with dates, but you may take it that the letter was written round about AD 60 from Paul's prison in Rome. The other thing to remember is this. The letter is about a runaway slave; and, to understand the situation, you should know that in those days a slave was reckoned as a mere chattel, a bit of his master's property. If he ran away, he could be sure of a severe flogging when he was caught, and might even have to pay for his folly with his life.

Behind the writing of this little letter of Paul lies a very moving human drama. The scene is laid first in Colossae, a town in Asia Minor 100 miles east of Ephesus, and then in Rome; and the three main characters in the drama are Paul, a citizen of Colossae named Philemon, and the runaway slave Onesimus. Here is what probably happened.

When, through Paul's preaching in Ephesus, the Gospel had penetrated inland to Colossae, among the first to believe were a well-to-do citizen named Philemon and his wife Apphia. Good Christians they were, for they provided a room in their house for their fellow-Christians to worship in, and kept open house for Christian travellers passing through. But about this time they had run into a bit of domestic trouble: one of their slaves, Onesimus, had helped himself to some of his master's money, and bolted.

Whither he went first we don't know; but eventually he turned up hundreds of miles away in Rome, drifting there no doubt as similar persons today might drift to London if they had 'money to burn'. At last, having spent all (like the prodigal) he found himself in the Capital of the world, 'homeless in the city, poor among the poor', when Providence took a strange but blessed hand in his affairs.

It chanced that about this time Paul had come to Rome to stand his trial as a Christian before the Emperor. One day the door of his prison opened to admit — Onesimus! How he found Paul we can't say; but we may imagine him blurting out his tale of shame, as we may also imagine Paul, after a kindly rebuke, beginning to tell Onesimus the Tale to whose telling he had given his life. The sequel was that Onesimus became a Christian and proved himself a great help to St Paul. But Paul, though he grew very fond of him, knew that it was his duty to send Onesimus back to his master when the opportunity offered. It came soon. One day there arrived a messenger from Colossae reporting the outbreak of heresy in the church there and requesting Paul's guidance.

So Paul sat down and wrote a letter to the Christians in Colossae — our Epistle to the Colossians — but before he put his pen away, he wrote another little letter to Philemon for Onesimus to take back with him. It is our letter, and in it Paul asks Philemon to give the runaway a gracious welcome back into his household, and even throws out a hint that he would like Philemon to release Onesimus for further Christian service with himself.

The fact that the letter has been preserved and included in the New Testament is evidence that Paul's plea did not fail. But did Philemon, besides forgiving Onesimus, release him for Christian service? Well, we know that some forty years later[1] there was a much beloved bishop in Ephesus named Onesimus, and it is no wild guess that he was the slave who had once run away. Onesimus had made good.

Now for the letter itself:

'From Paul, a prisoner of Christ Jesus and our colleague Timothy,' it begins, 'to our dear fellow-worker Philemon, our sister Apphia (his wife), our comrade-in-arms Archippus, and the congregation that meets in your house: grace and peace to you from God our Father and the Lord Jesus Christ.'

Then, very tactfully, Paul prepares the way for his chief point in writing:

'I always thank God when I mention you in my prayers; for, as I hear of your love and loyalty to the Lord Jesus and all God's people, I pray that by sharing in your faith they may have a vivid sense of how much good we Christians can achieve. I have been delighted and encouraged, brother Philemon, by your love and the way in which you have helped and refreshed God's people.'

Evidently some recent act of hospitality by Philemon had reached Paul's ears. He is glad to mention it because he is about to say something that will severely strain their friendship. Then, very delicately, he comes to the point:

'Hence, although I would feel quite free to *order* you to do your duty — because you owe your Christian faith to me — I much prefer to appeal to you for *love's* sake. Well then, as Paul the old man, who nowadays is a prisoner for

[1] Ignatius, writing to the Christians in Ephesus, refers to 'Onesimus your bishop, a man of inexpressible love'.

Christ's sake, I appeal to you for my spiritual son born to me in prison.'

We may imagine Philemon reading with pleasure and, as he comes to the last phrase, musing to himself: 'Spiritual son? I wonder who?'

At Paul's next word the secret is out: 'It is Onesimus!' (Here we should note that the name Onesimus means literally 'Useful', and then observe what happy play Paul makes with it.)

' "Useful" was anything but profitable to you in days gone by; but today he has become true to his name, very useful — to both you and me. I would fain have kept him, for in sending him back I feel I am parting with my own heart. But I did not want to do anything without your consent.

'Perhaps (Paul goes on) this was why you and he were parted for a while, that you might get him back for good, no longer as a mere slave but as something much more than a slave — a near brother, dear indeed to me and how much more to you, both as a man and as a Christian.'

Then comes the final appeal: 'You count me a partner? Then welcome him as you would myself. Ah but maybe you are still remembering the money he stole? Well, set it down to my account. Here's an IOU signed with my own hand, for the money. Come, brother, as a Christian be generous with me and relieve my anxiety. I am sending you this letter, confident that you will obey and do even more than I ask.'

Then, with a request to get lodgings ready for him, since he hopes soon to be freed, Paul sends greetings from all his friends — Mark and Luke among them — and ends with a blessing.

Two comments seem in place. First, Paul's letter to

Philemon has been called 'the *Magna Carta* of the slave'. To this it has been objected that Paul does not denounce the institution of slavery, here or in any other letter. Indeed, he does not. Little good such a denunciation would have done in a world where Christians had no vote, and there was little they could do short of bloody revolution. What they could do was to let the Gospel, through their own word and example, create such relations between master and slave that in time slavery would be seen in its own hideous light and abolished. The letter to Philemon is a good example of this Christian principle beginning its beneficent work.

Second: In Eph. 4: 15 Paul coins a splendid Greek phrase *alētheuōn en agapē*. Quite literally it means 'truthing it in love'. The letter to Philemon shows Paul practising what he preaches. It is a perfect example of truth, told lovingly. Truth is great, says the Roman proverb, and will prevail. Still greater is truth lovingly told, for it is Christian, and of God. Therefore, when you have a difficult letter to write or a disagreeable duty to perform, and you feel an urge to 'take it out of' the man who has offended you, let Paul come in your mind and 'truth it in love'.

FOR DISCUSSION

1. 'Persuasion is the only true intellectual process' (Matthew Arnold). In Philemon Paul persuades by Christian love. Is not this still the true Christian way? The Muslim is called to convert the enemies of Allah, if need be, at the point of the sword. In the Christian view,

God proposes to subdue his enemies by love, and we have no other weapons.

2. The congregation to which Philemon was written was a 'house-church'. Ought not the Church today to be experimenting more with 'house-churches' in order to spread the Gospel?

9. A Paean from Prison (Philippians)

From Paul's shortest letter we turn to what may well have been his last one, Philippians. Its four chapters contain many fine things; yet what is most remarkable in this letter from prison is its *radiance* — the words 'joy' or 'rejoice' occurring no fewer than 16 times.

Before we come to these things, however, we must answer a few questions.

First, to whom is the letter written? The first verse gives the answer: 'To all God's people incorporate in Christ Jesus who live at Philippi, together with the office-bearers there.' Philippi was a town in the northern part of Greece known as Macedonia, and took its name from Philip, father of Alexander the Great. Like Waterloo, it was famous as the scene of a decisive battle. Here, in 42 BC, the future Roman emperor Augustus had routed and slain the murderers of Julius Caesar. Some years later the Romans had turned Philippi into a Roman colony and settled some of their old soldiers in it.

To this historic town more than a century later (about AD 50), came Paul in the course of his second missionary journey, accompanied by Silas. You may read all about it in Acts 16. It was in Philippi that the local magistrates clapped Paul and Silas in gaol, putting their feet in the stocks. Yet, though they had a rough time in Philippi, they succeeded in founding a little church which by and by grew into a congregation of which Paul was prouder than any other. 'My joy and crown', he calls it in his letter (4: 1).

What prompted Paul to write it? You will find the answer in the closing paragraphs of chapter 4. Philippians was what we call nowadays a 'Thank You Letter'. When Paul wrote it, he was again in prison. Evidently news of his imprisonment had reached his friends in Philippi; whereupon, moved with sympathy, they 'put the hat round for him' (as we would say) and sent their present to him by the hand of one of their own members called Epaphroditus. 'It was kind of you to share my trouble,' Paul said in his letter of reply; and though he says he has learned to get along on very little, he was clearly touched by this practical token of their concern for their old father-in-God.

But where and when was Paul's letter written? Some modern scholars have conjectured that, though Acts says nothing about it, Paul was imprisoned in Ephesus, about AD 55, while he was evangelizing that great city. Now Paul's own letters (1 Cor. 15: 32; 2 Cor. 1: 8) make it clear that about this time Paul's life was in danger. Yet there is no clear, incontestable evidence that he was ever imprisoned in Ephesus. In questions like this where the burden of proof always rests on those who propound speculative theories, it is usually wiser to give the benefit of the doubt to tradition. And in the case of Paul's prison letters, like Philemon and Philippians, the tradition of the Church says that they came from his Roman prison. We may well accept it.

This enables us to date the letter. Paul, we know, reached Rome in AD 60, and lay in prison there for two years. Philippians was probably written towards the end of this time, and may well have been his 'swan song'.

Now let us go quickly through its four chapters. 'Dear Christians in Philippi,' he begins, 'I never remember you

E

without thankfulness, as I pray that you keep growing in Christian insight and knowledge. Let me assure you that my imprisonment has really been a blessing in disguise; for it has led to more preaching of Christ and a bolder Christian witness here; and though death might be better for me (for then I should see my Lord face to face) I believe I shall be spared to see you again' (chapter 1).

'By all your best Christian instincts, I urge you to be of one mind and heart, caring for each other's interests and not merely for your own. Take as your example our Lord himself who deliberately renounced the glories of heaven for you, to become a servant on earth and die upon a cross, so that God highly exalted him and gave him the highest name that heaven affords. Work out your own salvation — with God's help. If you do, I shall be proud of you on Judgment Day, even if now I have to die a martyr's death.

'Now about my plans. I am sending back our mutual friend Epaphroditus who has been critically ill here, and, later, my trusty colleague Timothy. Afterwards, if God will, I will come myself' (chapter 2).

'Meantime I wish you joy in the Lord. Give a wide berth to those Jewish brethren who think you must be circumcized if you are to be proper Christians. A sorry set of mutilators they are! Once upon a time I might have boasted myself a better Jew than any of them; but I said good-bye to all that when I met Christ and through faith in him found peace with God. So press on with me for the prize of God's high call in Christ; have no truck with the libertines in your midst; remember that we are a colony of heaven and that we wait for our Saviour who will change our lowly bodies into heavenly ones like his own' (chapter 3).

'I beg these two women in the congregation who have been at loggerheads to patch up their quarrel. Always be joyful; never stop saying your prayers; and take account of goodness wherever you find it.

'I was greatly heartened by your practical remembrance of me. I confess that experience has taught me how to do without, yet thank you for your gift, not the first I have had from you.

'All the brethren here send their good wishes, especially those who belong to the Emperor's Establishment.

'The grace of the Lord be with you.

Paul.' (chapter 4)

This bald summary does small justice to the richness of his letter. Why do we rate it so highly?

First, for the same reason that we value any good letter from a dear friend. *It reveals the man himself.* Some people have the happy knack of setting themselves down on paper so that we can almost hear them speaking. Paul was like this, and from Philippians you will learn a lot about the man Paul. If you have imagined him as a pretty grim old chap, you are in for a surprise. What we find in Philippians is a warm-hearted, very courageous, and indomitably cheerful man.

The next reason for prizing Philippians is that *it contains at least three famous passages.* In the first, Phil. 2: 6–11, Paul quotes what was probably the earliest Christian hymn. It has six stanzas, each of three lines. Here it is in modern translation:

> Though in God's form he was,
> Christ Jesus would not snatch
> At parity with God.

Himself he sacrificed,
Taking a servant's form,
Being born like every man;

Revealed in human shape,
Obediently he stooped
To die upon a cross.

Him therefore God raised high,
Gave him the name of Lord,
All other names above;

That, at the Saviour's name,
No knee might be unbowed,
In heaven, or earth, or hell;

And every tongue confess,
To God the Father's praise,
That 'Jesus Christ is Lord'.[1]

The second celebrated passage is 3: 4–11. Here Paul describes the great renunciation he made of all his Jewish privileges when he became a Christian. He lists them all as if he were ticking them off on his fingers. Then, having collected them, as it were, into one parcel, he tells how he wrote 'Loss' across it when he met the risen Christ and came to know him as Saviour.

The third passage is Phil. 4: 8. Examine it, and you will find it full of words that might have come from some contemporary manual of Greek moral philosophy: truth, virtue, merit and so on. Evidently his readers had asked Paul what attitude they should adopt to the good features in the pagan society around them. Paul's answer is a noble one:

[1] *The Church Hymnary* (*Third Edition*), Hymn 399.

'All that rings true,' he says, 'all that commands reverence, and all that makes for right: all that is pure, all that is attractive, all that is high-toned: virtue and merit, wherever these are found, you must take them into your account.'

May we not learn here? When in our day-to-day contacts with our neighbours — humanists, communists, or ordinary pagans — we encounter goodness and truth, should we not be quick to acknowledge it? For is not God, in Christ's view (Mark 10: 18), the ultimate source of all goodness?

Finally, *Philippians lets us into the deepest secret of the Christian life.* Sometimes we say, 'Christianity is Christ.' But what kind of Christ? When some people talk about him, you get the impression that Christ is just a figure in an old, old story who lived 1900 years ago in Palestine, dazzled men for a year or two by his wonderful works and words, and then left the world for ever. Paul does not talk about him this way. His Christ is a living person with whom he is in touch every day. 'For me to live is Christ,' he says (1: 21) and, again, 'I can do all things in Christ who strengthens me' (4: 13). Paul talks about his independence; but the secret of his independence is his dependence on Another. It is the secret also of his serenity.

During World War Two, just after Martin Niemöller, once a famous U-boat commander, had been put in a concentration camp because he chose to obey God rather than Hitler, I remember being allowed to read a letter he wrote to an Oxford friend of mine. 'In the old days,' he wrote, 'I used to be a bearer of the Gospel. Now that Gospel is bearing me.' This sentence and the serenity of the whole letter are all I now recall; but when I read it it reminded me of nothing so much as Paul to the

Philippians. 'I rejoice,' says Paul, 'and you must rejoice too.' Philippians is not so much a letter as a paean from prison. It is a perpetual reminder to all us lesser Christians that long faces are a poor advertisement for our faith, and that in any true Christianity 'cheerfulness should always keep breaking in'.

FOR DISCUSSION

1. 'It is my prayer that your love may abound more and more, with knowledge and all discernment' (1: 9). Which is more important in a Christian congregation — increase in members and money, or growth in Christian love and true understanding of the Faith?

2. 'Work out your own salvation with fear and trembling,' Paul says (2: 12f.), 'for God is at work in you, both to will and work for his good pleasure.' How can these two assertions be reconciled? According to the logicians, only one of two contraries can be true. But in the reality of the Christian life may not *both* Paul's statements be true?

10. The Epistle of Priesthood (Hebrews)

About the time the Roman general Agricola was subduing our rude forefathers in this land, there began to circulate in the young Church a little religious masterpiece. It had no title, but soon acquired one — 'To the Hebrews.' For the most part it was a finely-phrased discourse arguing that Christ was the perfect Priest, but it ended like a letter, with brief news and greetings. Unfortunately, the author did not put his name to it, or that of his readers, or tell us plainly why he wrote. Yet in his thirteen chapters he lets fall some clues. Let us see what we can make of them.

I

Who was the Writer? The Authorized Version says he was St Paul. But ancient opinion was divided for and against Paul's authorship, and modern scholars agree that the thought and style are not his. Yet Heb. 13: 23 ('You should know that our brother Timothy has been released') indicates that he was of Paul's circle. Who then? In Acts 18: 24f., Luke describes Paul's colleague Apollos thus: 'A Jew, an Alexandrian by birth, an eloquent man, powerful in his use of the scriptures.' Apollos was therefore (1) a Jew who had become a Christian; (2) an eloquent preacher; (3) a native of Alexandria; and (4) an expert in the Old Testament. Now this four-fold description fits the Writer to the Hebrews like a glove. He was a Jewish

Christian. His rhetorical style betrays the preacher. He interprets Christianity in terms of the Platonic philosophy current in Alexandria. He makes massive use of the Old Testament, sometimes allegorizing it as the Alexandrian Jew Philo did. If then we are to put a name on the title-page of Hebrews, 'the best bet' is Apollos. And if not Apollos, then, spiritually speaking, his twin brother.

Where did his readers live? The case for locating them in Rome is strong. The letter is first quoted there, about AD 95, by Clement, bishop of Rome. Clement and our Writer use the same Greek word to describe the church's leaders (*hēgoumenoi*). Timothy was known in Rome (Col. 1: 1, Philem. 1). And the phrase 'those who hail from Italy' (13: 34) probably points in the same direction.

What kind of Christians were they? They were Jewish Christians who, threatened by persecution, would fain have crept back under the shelter of Judaism, a religion permitted by Rome as Christianity was not. Living too much in the Jewish part of their faith, they were remaining backwardly blind to the far horizons of their Christian calling. By contrast, the Writer of Hebrews was a man of the same bold, forward-looking vision as Stephen the first martyr. Like Stephen, he had glimpsed the universal dominion of the Son of Man (compare Acts 7: 56 with Dan. 7: 13f.) and knew that the New Israel, the Church, was destined to world-mission.

This view explains many things in Hebrews: the Writer's warning against 'drifting' from their Christian course (2: 1–4); his insistence in the key chapters of his letter (7–10: 18) that the new means of grace brought by Christ offers the reality which Judaism could only fore-shadow; his caution against 'shrinking back' (10: 38f.); his summons in chapter 11 to the pilgrim life of faith;

and his challenge in chapter 13 to 'go forth to Jesus outside the camp, bearing the stigma that he bore' (13: 13 NEB).

The letter was probably written before AD 70 when the Romans destroyed the Temple in Jerusalem. Had the Temple fallen before he wrote, he must have pointed to its fall as proof conclusive that God had no further use for this focus of the ancient sanctities. The letter mentions *two* persecutions: one past, one pending. The first (10: 32f.) probably describes the trouble in the Roman synagogues when the Gospel found entrance there and the Emperor Claudius expelled the Jews from Rome (Acts 18: 2. Date, AD 49). The second (12: 3ff.) suggests the first moves against the Christians which issued in the Neronian blood-bath of AD 64. A date about AD 63 seems likely.

II

Now to the letter itself. It falls into two parts: (1) The main argument (1: 1–10: 18) and (2) the closing exhortation (10: 19–13: 25).

The Main Argument

First, in his prologue, the Writer declares that, in contrast to the Old Testament revelation which was fragmentary, God has now in this 'final age' made a complete revelation of himself in his Son. Then he proves Christ greater than the angels through whom, tradition said, the Law had been given (chapters 1–2). (In 2: 1–4 he pauses to warn his readers against 'drifting' from their Christian moorings.) Next, he shows Christ superior to Moses, as a son is superior to a servant in God's household (3: 1–6). (Again he digresses in 3: 7 to 4: 13 to warn his readers against missing God's promised 'rest'.) Eventually he reaches his

main theme — the high-priesthood of Christ — and finds
fulfilled in Christ the two chief qualifications of a high-
priest: sympathy with those he represents and divine
appointment (4: 14–5: 10). (Once again, in 5: 11–6: 12,
he stops to warn his readers against backsliding.) Then,
at 6: 13, he resumes his main argument.

In chapter 7 Christ is shown to belong to a higher order
of priesthood, represented not by Aaron but by the
primeval priest Melchizedek (Gen. 14: 18–20, Psalm
110: 4), and the Levitical priesthood is superseded by that
of Christ, the ideal high-priest.

In chapter 8 he shows that Christ, the ideal high-priest,
ministers in an ideal sanctuary, heaven itself, and his
ministry has meant the establishment of the new covenant
between God and man prophesied in Jer. 31: 31ff.

In chapter 9 he shows that Christ, the ideal high priest,
offers the perfect sacrifice for sins; and his argument ends
with the proof of the futility of Jewish sacrifice and the
finality of Christ's 'single sacrifice for sins' (10: 1–18).

The Closing Exhortation

He begins by urging his readers to avail themselves of 'the
new and living way' opened up by Christ into God's
presence, warning them of the danger of backsliding.
Then, praising their earlier fortitude in persecution, he
reminds them that they stand in the succession of the
heroes of faith (10: 19–11: 40). Their suffering, he says,
is evidence of God's fatherly discipline, and he powerfully
contrasts the glories of the New Covenant with the terrors
of the Old one (chapter 12). The last chapter bids them
imitate their leaders, warns against strange teachings,
and ends with a noble doxology and greetings (chapter
13).

III

Much in this masterpiece sounds strangely on our ears today. Let us try to catch its main drift.

A picture in Catterick Camp, painted during World War One, shows a signaller lying dead in No-man's-land. He had been sent out to repair a cable broken by shell-fire. There he lies, cold in death but with his task fulfilled; for in his stiffening hands he holds the cable's broken ends, *together*. Beneath the picture stands one word: THROUGH.

This is a parable of what our Writer is saying. Basically, the Christian religion means man entering into friendship with God — a friendship made possible by what God has done in Christ. Before Christ, men were at odds with God, because their sin had snapped the contact between God and man. Christ, by his self-sacrifice, has repaired the broken friendship between God and man.

For our Writer, religion means primarily *access* to God through worship. What hinders it and impairs that communion with God for which man was made is sin. If man is ever to attain it, he must somehow 'get through' to God. But how? The ritual of Judaism — the whole system of priest and sanctuary and sacrifice — professed to take him there. Alas, it could not. Cleanse the *flesh* it might, but the *conscience* stained with sin it could not. Christianity is the final religion because, through Christ's self-sacrifice, it secures that access to God which Judaism could only shadow forth. With Christ we pass 'out of the shadows into the truth'.

This is the theme of Hebrews; and using Plato's two-storeyed view of the world — the Shadowy and the Real — our Writer shows how Christ our high priest, by his sacrifice, has pioneered a way into the Holy of Holies, which is heaven. So we Christians are able, in virtue of Christ's sacrifice, to pass by faith, here and now, into the heavenly world and commune with 'the Father of spirits'. (Michael Bruce, the Loch Leven poet, has given us the heart of the matter in his hymn: 'Where high the heavenly temple stands.')

And the relevance of Hebrews for us today? First, in these days when 'the world is too much with us', we need to hear its *pilgrim* note — sounded most clearly in chapter 11. The heroes there depicted, from Abraham to the Maccabees, are men in search of the true fatherland of their spirits. The badge they wear is faith which is a 'venturing on vision'. In Jesus, 'the pioneer and perfecter of faith' (12: 2), the end of their quest is to be seen. He is faith's mightiest captain who has blazed the trail and opened up a new way whereby we too may travel to that City of our soul's desiring.

The second note is *ecumenical*. If we will, Hebrews will teach us the unwisdom of clinging to the old securities when the clarion call is for men to carry Christ's empire to the ends of the earth. For the Church becomes truly the Church when, refusing to be merely an ark of refuge for the faithful, it goes out into the world to claim it for God and His Christ.

The third note, that of the *unchanging Christ*, is a corollary of the second. We hear it in Heb. 13: 7f. 'Remember your leaders, those who spoke to you the word of God: consider the outcome of their life and imitate their faith. Jesus Christ is the same, yesterday, today and for ever.'

Their first fathers in the faith had gone to their reward, leaving them noble examples to follow. But over their Lord death had no power. *Yesterday* he had lived and suffered and died for their sins. *Today* and *for ever* he lives in God's eternal Kingdom, 'the Saviour and the Friend of man'.

But the readers of Hebrews had to learn that, though their Christ was unchanging, he was also onward-moving, ever calling his people to fresh adventures of faith. How hard it was for them to adjust to life in that changing world of theirs, and yet outside, *in* that changing world was their changeless Lord bidding them 'go forth' to him 'outside the camp'.

Today we too live in a world where the old landmarks are fast disappearing. In face of all the uncertainties we also are tempted to sit tight in the old camps and hug the old ways. Yet this is not God's will for us in Christ. We need the ministry of the unchanging but ever onward-moving Christ. If we belong to 'a Kingdom which cannot be shaken' (12: 28), yet the revelation we have in Christ is dynamic, is ever calling us to new dimensions of Christian thought and action. Much land still remains to be possessed in the name of Christ. We are summoned to go forward in the steps of this unchanging but always onward-moving Christ —

> 'On to the end of the road,
> On to the City of God.'

FOR DISCUSSION

1. The word 'priest' has no place in the religious thinking of some Protestants. But if a priest is 'somebody worthy to stand before God, to offer spiritual sacrifices, and to pray for men', have we not a right to think of Christ the Son

doing this for us before his Father? (Read William Bright's great hymn 'And now, O Father'.)

2. 'The Lord hath yet more light and truth to break forth from his holy Word' (John Robinson of Pilgrim Fathers fame). Discuss this in the light of the teaching of Hebrews.

11. The Epistle of Hope (1 Peter)

R. L. Stevenson somewhere recalls a conversation he had with a Fife labourer who was cleaning a byre (or cowshed). Their talk ran on many things, but especially the aims and ends of life. And, as they conversed, the labourer let fall one remark that revealed the man: 'Him that has aye something ayont need never be weary.' That man had caught the accents of 1 Peter. It is the epistle of hope, not a mere wistful hoping for the best but Christian hope — that confident anticipation of a heavenly inheritance resting on the God who raised Jesus from the dead and 'gave him glory that our faith and hope might be in him'.

It was to keep the lamp of hope burning in dark days that the letter was written. But what dark days were these? Who were the Christians who needed this call to hope and fortitude, and does Peter indeed stand behind this letter?

I

'Peter an apostle of Jesus Christ,' the letter begins. Three verses from its end we read: 'I write this brief appeal to you through Silvanus, our trusty brother, as I hold him.' (5: 12). Silvanus is the Silas associated with Paul in Acts, and named by him at the beginning of his two letters to Thessalonica. First Peter then purports to be the work of the apostle Peter with the help of Silvanus, a prominent and able man in the early Church.

Though some modern men have questioned it, Peter's connection with the letter was never doubted in the early Church. A study of the letter's contents would seem to confirm tradition. The writer claims to have been 'a witness of Christ's sufferings' (5: 1) and also 'a partaker of the splendour that is to be revealed' — which sounds like a reference to Christ's transfiguration. He seems to betray first-hand knowledge of the trial of Jesus, for he writes, 'When he was reviled, he did not revile in return; when he suffered, he did not threaten, but he trusted to him who judges justly' (2: 23). In his letters he quotes, or echoes, about a dozen sayings of Jesus. All this supports Peter's connection with our letter. Moreover, on various points of detail, e.g. the conception of Jesus as the suffering Servant of the Lord and the description of the Cross as a 'tree',[1] we find parallels between the letter and the speeches of Peter reported in the Acts of the Apostles.

We may therefore accept the early Church's ascription of the letter to St Peter, only adding that Silvanus's contribution to it probably went a good deal beyond the mere labour of writing.

Who were the recipients of the letter? Answer: 'the elect of the Dispersion in Pontus, Galatia, Cappadocia, Asia and Bithynia' (1: 1). These were Roman provinces in Asia Minor (which you should pick out on a good map of the ancient world). But why the word 'Dispersion'? This commonly signified in those days the Jews living in Gentile lands outside Palestine, but it cannot have this meaning here. The letter shows that Peter's readers were largely Gentiles (1: 14, 18 and 4: 3), and there can be no doubt that the people addressed are recently-converted Gentile Christians in Asia Minor, forming part of the true people

[1] I Peter 2: 24; Acts 5: 30. Cf. Deut. 21: 23.

of God scattered abroad in an alien world. First Peter is therefore what we would nowadays call an *encyclical letter* to the Christians in the above-mentioned Roman provinces.

Where was it written? The clue is to be found in 1 Peter 5: 13: 'She who is in Babylon ... sends you greetings.' 'She' by general consent refers to the church from which Peter was writing. But 'Babylon'? Can this be the once famous city on the Euphrates? It cannot. There is nothing to connect Peter with the Babylon of the celebrated Hanging Gardens, but there is excellent tradition connecting him with Rome. So nowadays it is agreed that 'Babylon' in First Peter is what it is in the book of Revelation, a cryptic name for Rome.

When did Peter write from Rome? Both Paul and Peter perished in the Neronian persecution which broke out in AD 64 but was beginning to 'hot up' a few years earlier. Accordingly a date about AD 63 would fit the facts implied in the letter. It is still possible to advise loyalty to the Roman empire (2: 13), and the language of the letter suggests an impending rather than an actual persecution. We may therefore take it that 1 Peter was written shortly before AD 64 when the trouble brewing in the Capital was threatening to spread to Rome's provinces, and that therefore Peter used 'Babylon' as a precautionary pseudonym for Rome.

II

Now for the contents of the letter. After the opening address (already discussed) and a noble doxology for the risen Christ, Peter describes the fulfilment of Old Testament prophecy in the Gospel of their salvation and bids his readers respond to it by holy living (1: 1–2: 3).

As the people (or temple) of God, of which Christ is the living Head, they are summoned to a service which is both priestly — to offer up spiritual sacrifices — and prophetic — to tell out the triumphs of the God who has called them out of darkness into light (2: 4–10).

Peter then instructs them in various patterns of Christian social behaviour (2: 11–3: 12), before facing them with the prospect of persecution: if and when it comes, they should endure it in the spirit of Christ and live as Christians should by the will of God (3: 13–4: 6). In this time of crisis let them use their various gifts for God's glory and the good of their fellows (4: 7–11). The ordeal of persecution should not surprise them; rather should they count it all joy to suffer for Christ's sake, though never as malefactors or mischief-makers (4: 12–19).

As a fellow-elder, Peter bids the elders in their midst tend their flocks faithfully, in hope of the Chief Shepherd's reward (5: 1–5). Let them be humble, vigilant, steadfast, always relying on the gracious God who has called them to glory (5: 6–11).

Then, with a mention of his scribe Silvanus and 'his son Mark' he sends greetings, and ends with a blessing: 'Peace to you all who belong to Christ.'

III

First Peter is one of the finest things in the New Testament and 'worthy', as John Calvin said, 'of the chief of the apostles'. Steadfastness in persecution is one of its main themes. Another is the need for good Christian behaviour, so that the suspicions of pagan neighbours may be disarmed and the Christian Way commended (2: 12). But the letter's dominant theme is the summons to Christian

hope in dark days. 'Blessed are they,' said Jesus, 'who are
persecuted for righteousness' sake, for theirs is the kingdom
of heaven' — a Beatitude which Peter himself quotes
(3: 14). There is no better commentary on the beatitude
than this noble letter. Here is no grey and close-lipped
Stoicism which can only grin and bear it. Here rather is
an apostolic document which has caught the true temper
of the Christ who 'for the joy that was set before him,
endured the Cross, despising the shame, and is set down
at the right hand of the throne of God' — a document
which, though the skies are dark and the enemy menacing,
glows with that hope of 'an inheritance which is
imperishable, undefiled and unfading, kept in heaven for
you who by God's power are guarded through faith for a
salvation ready to be revealed in the last time' (1: 4f.).

May we not say that any man who really has a hope like
this need 'never be weary'?

FOR DISCUSSION

1. In the dawn of Christianity 'the blood of the martyrs
was the seed of the Church'. Might not a spot of
persecution be a good thing for the Church's reviving
today?

2. 'Faith, hope, love, these three. . . .' We Christians have
made much of faith and talked plenty about love (though
often failing to practise it). Is not hope the real Cinderella
among the three Christian graces today?

12. The Judgment and Victory of God (Revelation)

The last book in the New Testament is the strangest, as it has long been a happy hunting ground for cranks. To the ordinary reader, it is like a tunnel with light at the beginning and light at the end, and in the middle 'a long stretch of darkness through which lurid objects thunder past, bewildering and stunning the reader'. 'What on earth (or in heaven),' he asks, 'is it all about?' The true answer is that it is about the judgment and victory of God. But if this is to become clear, we had better begin at the beginning and do some explaining.

I. *Apocalypses and the Apocalypse*

Revelation is the finest Christian example of an apocalypse. 'Apocalypse' means 'unveiling', and apocalypses are writings which undertake to 'unveil' the last things and reveal the final issue of God's purpose. (Many of us have an apocalyptic streak in our make-up — like the little lass who, on being told that 'Granny had gone to be with God' exclaimed, 'Gosh! How posh!' Somehow she divined that, though it had been sad about 'Gran', it was going to be all right now that she had gone to be with 'the Good Man Above'.)

Apocalypses, of which the Jews wrote many in the two centuries before Christ, represent the search for an interpretation of history which will embrace catastrophe and transcend present tragedy. Born in bad times, they are written to fortify the faithful in their ordeal by letting them see the consummation of God's purpose. Inevitably, they take the form of *visions* — visions of what lies beyond the doom-dark horizons of history.

But why should the imagery of an apocalypse be so fantastic, its scenery so 'out of this world'? One reason is that these books attempt to peer into the undisclosed future, and it is only in the language of symbol that we can describe what eye has not seen nor ear heard. The other reason is that apocalypses appear in a time when freedom of speech is in eclipse. Your 'apocalyptist' dare not deal in plain speech: he must wrap up his message in a kind of cypher language to which he hopes his readers will have the key. Thus the writer of Revelation deliberately refers to Rome as 'Babylon'.

And so to 'The Revelation of St John the Divine', as the Authorized Version calls it.

The book was written about AD 95 when the Roman emperor Domitian had begun to persecute the Christians in real earnest. His excuse for harrying them was 'emperor worship'. In its origin this was an attempt to bind together the far-flung Roman empire by giving it a common religion, namely, the worship by all its citizens of the emperor as 'Our Lord and God'. Now Domitian took this very seriously and rigorously enforced the Caesar-cult (as it is called) in Asia Minor where the seven churches of Asia lay. Statues of the emperor were set up, priests appointed, and the subject peoples commanded to accord divine honours to Domitian.

Christ or Caesar? A very serious issue this was for the sincere Christian. For him, one only deserved the title of 'Lord', and yet to defy the imperial edict was to court banishment and even death. Our writer had in fact defied it and found himself exiled to the lonely Aegean isle of Patmos where the Romans kept political prisoners. Here he saw the visions recorded in his book.

Who was he? He was a Jewish Christian named John (1: 4, 9); but if style is any test, he was not the John of the Gospel and the three epistles. John the evangelist writes with the profound simplicity of a Bunyan; the prophet of Patmos has the forked-lightning style of a Carlyle describing the French Revolution. The authoritative tone of his book shows him to have been a prominent church leader in Asia. To distinguish him from the evangelist, and to describe his special gift, we often call him 'John the Seer'.

II. *The Divine Drama*

His book takes the form of a circular letter meant to be read to the seven churches of Asia named in chapters 2 and 3 (Ephesus, Smyrna, Pergamum and the rest). But it is best regarded as a *drama* of divine judgment and victory. For the materials of his book John has drawn on his own visions, the Old Testament and various other sources; but all are skilfully interwoven and the drama flames to its climax in the destruction of 'Babylon' (Rome) and the vindication of God's people (the Church). After the Prologue and the letters to the seven churches in the first three chapters, the bulk of the book is taken up with the judgment and victory of God (4: 1–22: 5), before it ends with an Epilogue, invoking a curse on all who tamper with his book and a prayer for the coming of Christ (22: 6–21).

Before describing the drama, let us note two dramatic features of the author's style.

First, one of John's devices is the *principle of parenthesis, or interlude*. Just as a musician may introduce a light movement between two very sombre ones, so John, when his visions of judgment become almost unbearable, relieves the tension by switching the scene from the agonies of earth to the beatitude of heaven. There is one such interlude in chapter 7 where, right in the middle of the seven seals of judgment, we are given a glimpse of the redeemed in glory.

A second feature of apocalypses is *double happenings* — events in heaven which have their counterparts on earth. Thus in 12: 7ff. Michael's defeat of Satan in heaven is the counterpart of Christ's earthly triumph over evil on the Cross.

But now to the drama itself. After the Prologue and the letters to the seven churches, at 4: 1 the curtain rises and the revelation proper begins. Through an open door in heaven John sees the ineffable God on his throne worshipped by the heavenly hosts. In his hand is a *scroll* fastened with seven seals — the book of God's plan for the world. One only is found worthy to open it, a Lamb 'with the marks of slaughter on him' — obviously the crucified and glorified Christ. With the opening of the sealed book the visions of judgment begin.

First come the judgments inaugurated by the breaking of the seven seals (chapters 6 and 8: 1). Four horsemen ride forth to spread havoc in the earth. With the breaking of the fifth seal the martyrs are heard calling on God to vindicate them. They are given white robes and told to 'rest a little longer'. The sixth seal brings a world-wide earthquake, and with the seventh — after that glimpse of the redeemed in heaven — comes 'a brief silence in heaven'; but it is only the lull before the gathering storm.

After the seven seals come the seven *trumpets* (chapters 8–9). The first six herald hail on the earth, fire in the sea, poison in the rivers, the eclipse of the heavenly bodies, and so on. Then, after two obscure passages, the seventh trumpet sounds (11: 15) and a great shout is heard in heaven: 'The sovereignty has passed to our Lord and his Christ, and he shall reign for ever and ever!'

With chapter 12, in what we would call a 'flash-back', there appears a woman (the Church) giving birth to a Child (Christ) who is menaced by a Dragon (the Devil). When the Child is caught up into heaven, the Dragon pursues him thither, only to be cast out by Michael and the angels. Then, on earth, the Dragon attacks the Woman's offspring, helped by two Beasts. The first (the Roman Empire) wars on God's people, while the second one (the local Caesar-cult) serves as his bestial accomplice.

With chapter 14 comes another heavenly interlude, in which John sees the Church Triumphant and the Son of Man in power. Then angel after angel announces the coming harvest of judgment.

In chapters 15 and 16 angels go forth with the seven *bowls* of God's wrath. The first four ruin land, sea, rivers and sun; the fifth plunges the beast's realm in darkness; and when the sixth is outpoured, the kings of the earth muster for Armageddon, the last great battle between God and the forces of evil. The seventh bowl brings an earthquake devastating the cities.

With chapters 17 and 18 we approach the climax. In vision John sees Babylon (Rome) as a great harlot astride a beast and drunk with the blood of the saints. Then he hears 'great Babylon's doom pronounced by heaven's command', while the kings of the earth, the merchants and the sea-captains lament her fall.

The resultant Hallelujahs in heaven have hardly died away when Christ, the Word of God, rides forth on a white horse to vanquish the Beast and his worshippers (chapter 19).

The conquering Christ now reigns on earth with his martyrs for a thousand years. Then the Devil, who has been imprisoned, is let loose for his final attack on God's people; and after his defeat and consignment to a lake of fire, comes the Last Judgment (chapter 20).

Finally, with the darkness of Doomsday past, we emerge from 'the tunnel' into the light. Like a new Moses, John stands on his Pisgah peak and surveys the promised land. With the old heaven and earth gone, he is granted a glimpse of 'the holy city, the new Jerusalem' where 'the Lord God will be their light' and they shall reign for ever and ever' (chapters 21–22: 5). Then follows the Epilogue (22: 6–21).

III. *Its Interpretation*

How do we interpret this tremendous book?

The first principle is: *Interpret it in the light of the times when it was written*. Never treat it as an Old Moore's Almanac replete with allusions to persons and events lying, so to speak, in the womb of the distant future. Thus the beast whose number is 666 (13: 18) is not Hitler, but probably the wicked emperor Nero who, rumour had it, had come back to life and resumed his devilry.

Second: *avoid a crude literalism*. For instance, the last two chapters are not a divinely-inspired ordnance map of heaven. When John depicts the heavenly Jerusalem as a cube-shaped city of gold, having twelve gates and walls 1500 feet high, his interest is not in statistics but in symbols.

What he is trying to suggest is the indescribable magnitude and perfection of 'Jerusalem the Golden'. Here John's meaning has been best caught not by the celestial map-makers but by poets like St Bernard in his hymn.

Third: in order to understand Revelation, *you need some knowledge of John's mystic numbers.* (This should not be altogether strange to us who regard 3 as lucky and 13 as unlucky.) For John, 3 is the number of heaven, 4 of earth, and 7 the perfect number. 12 is the church number. It provides the clue to the 144,000 persons who have been sealed for salvation in chapter 7: 4. For 144,000 is 12 times 12 multiplied by 1000. By it John means us to think of the vast completeness of God's redeemed people.

The fourth principle of interpretation (to be explained in a moment) may be called that of '*the backside of the wall*'. but, first, go back to Rev. 1: 3 where John declares: 'The crisis (*kairos*) is near.' This is not (though many have so taken it) the end of the world but the persecution of the Church. This crisis John sets against the backdrop of the supreme crisis — Doomsday — in order to show Christian martyrs the real nature of their suffering and its place in God's eternal purpose. Now recall an episode in *The Pilgrim's Progress*. Visiting the Interpreter's House, Christian is perplexed to see a fire burning against a wall, a fire which flames still higher when a man apparently throws water on it. His puzzlement ends only when the Interpreter takes him to 'the backside of the wall' where he sees a man with a jug of *oil* in his hand. Just so, according to John the Seer, *history has a backroom* into which the man of faith can look and see the inner meaning of the events through which he lives. John's aim is therefore to show 'the backside of the wall' to Christians who may be dragged before their Roman persecutors. They are to know that their suffering is a part of God's eternal purpose, attested by his Christ (1:2), 'a purpose as old as the world and as ultimate as the crack of doom'.[1]

Read thus, Revelation acquires a relevance for us today.

IV. *Relevance*

To begin with, Revelation is *a message for a crisis*. Ours is certainly such an age, both for the world and the church. In this century evil has been unleashed in the world on a scale unprecedented in history, and in many lands Christians have suffered persecution and even martyrdom. Inevitably the hearts of many have failed them for fear of what is coming on the earth. So this strange book, now nineteen centuries old, can again become a trumpet-call to steadfast faith in time of calamity.

Next, *Revelation is a noble affirmation of true Christian optimism*. Christian optimism, like John's, is no facile, fair-weather optimism which has never known 'the cloudy and dark day'. Rather is it a 'beyond-tragedy' optimism, an optimism which has looked into the very abyss of evil unaffrighted — unaffrighted because it knows that the world belongs to God and not to the devil. This world, John believes, with all its blessings as God's handiwork, and with all its evils as the fruit of man's sins, is still the venue of God's redemptive purpose. The key to its mystery is Christ, the glorified Lamb of God, who having died to redeem the race, now reigns with God. Because of Christ's victory over evil on the Cross, John knows that the evil world cannot win at last because it failed to win the only

[1] I owe this illustration to G. B. Caird, author of the best modern commentary on Revelation.

time it ever could. Despite all appearances, it is a vanquished world in which men play their devilries.

Finally, *Revelation is an abiding witness to the reality of heaven.* More than any other New Testament writer, John the Seer has power to infect us with his own certitude of the unseen and eternal world (see 7: 13–17; 21: 1–4; 22: 1–5). As he assured his first readers, so he can assure us that at the end of the Christian road there is a city — the City of God; that, whatever else heaven means, it means an end to the sorrows of earth; and that the last reward of the loyal and pure in heart will be to see God and his Christ face to face in the presence of all the redeemed.

'They shall see his face,' he promises, 'and his name shall be on their foreheads. And night shall be no more, they need no light of lamp or sun, for the Lord God will be their light, and they shall reign for ever and ever' (22: 4f.).

Thus, fitly, does John the Seer end his revelation — and the New Testament — with the Beatific Vision and a Hallelujah chorus.

FOR DISCUSSION

1. Luther wished to exclude this book from the New Testament, and some have thought that there is nothing Christian about it. Is this a fair judgment?

2. Why are those people misguided who think to find in Revelation a detailed forecast of future world-history?

Epilogue

Gospels, Acts, Epistles, Apocalypse — what a variety of literary forms we have in the little library of the New Testament! Yes, and sometimes — until we understand what they mean — how different seem their various themes — the Kingdom of God (Gospels), reconciliation to God in Christ (Paul), eternal life (John) etc.

Yet beneath this diversity of form and content lies a basic unity of message. To put it musically: if in the New Testament there are many musicians playing different instruments, one fundamental theme runs through all their music-making. It is the story of how —

> 'A Second Adam to the fight
> And to the rescue came.'

The story has three elements: a Saviour (who is Christ the Lord), a saved (and saving) People of God, and the work of salvation. These form three strands in a single cord — a trinity in unity — and their unity makes up the New Testament's Good News of God's rescue of our fallen race in Christ.[1]

It begins in eternity, as it ends in eternity, and its centre

[1] For a fuller exposition of the unity of the New Testament see my *Introducing the New Testament* (SCM Press), pp. 198–208. There readers will also find 'introductions' to all the other New Testament documents inevitably omitted in this little book.

in time is a Cross on a Hill and an Empty Tomb. This New Testament message is 'the Word from the Beyond for our human predicament' of which we spoke at the beginning. It is the record of God's saving activity in Christ incarnate, crucified, risen, regnant, and yet to come in glory. And its purpose and meaning are best summed up in the words of St John:

'God so loved the world that he gave his only Son that whoever believes in him should not perish but have eternal life' (John 3: 16).

Is that not still Good News for sin-sick and bewildered modern man?